The Rule of Love

broken, fulfilled, and applied

J. V. Fesko

Reformation Heritage Books

Grand Rapids, Michigan

The Rule of Love
Copyright © 2009 J. V. Fesko

Published by
Reformation Heritage Books
2965 Leonard St., NE
Grand Rapids, MI 49525
616-977-0599 / Fax 616-285-3246
e-mail: orders@heritagebooks.org
website: www.heritagebooks.org

Library of Congress Cataloging-in-Publication Data

Fesko, J. V., 1970-
  The rule of love : broken, fulfilled, and applied / J.V. Fesko.
      p. cm.
ISBN 978-1-60178-063-8 (hardcover : alk. paper) 1. Ten
commandments—Criticism, interpretation, etc. 2. Bible. O.T.
Exodus XX, 2–17—Criticism, interpretation, etc. 3. Law and
gospel. I. Title.
BS1245.52.F47 2009
222'.1606—dc22

                                    2009014419

To

David and Susan Winslow

*For their
tireless service
to Christ and His church*

Contents

Acknowledgements

This little book originally began with a sermon series on the Book of Exodus. As the sermons were shaped into a book, my parents, brother, in-laws, and several friends read through various manuscripts. I truly appreciated their feedback. My wife also gave me helpful suggestions as we talked about the book in the car or at the dinner table. I am especially indebted to my friends Wally King and Dave Van Drunen for reading the entire manuscript and giving me helpful critique and feedback. Many thanks are due to Jay T. Collier, who also read the manuscript and encouraged me to publish it with Reformation Heritage Books. I am grateful, therefore, for Jay and the staff at Reformation Heritage for all of their work in preparing this book for publication.

There is a saying, "Behind every great man is a great woman." The first part of this saying does not apply to me, but the second part certainly applies to my beautiful wife, Anneke. I am profoundly grateful for her unwavering love, encouragement, and support. She not only cares for and loves me but also for our young son, Val. Anneke, thank you for your love and encouragement.

I first heard of David and Susan Winslow's tireless work with covenant youth of the Orthodox Presbyterian Church by word of mouth and later through my wife, who went on two Backpacking Adventures in the High Sierras led by the Winslows when my wife was in college. What amazes me is David's ability to remember by name each college and high school student who went with him and Susan in more than twenty years of backpacking trips. They typically led two trips per year. I saw David and Susan's devotion firsthand, as my wife and I accompanied them on a backpacking trip in the summer of 2005, when I used this material for daily devotions. I also witnessed firsthand their indefatigable labors on behalf of the church. They have set a Christ-honoring example of what Paul says about the goal of the Law: "Love worketh no ill to his neighbour: therefore love is the fulfilling of the law" (Rom. 13:10). So, it is to David and Susan Winslow, a dear brother and sister in Christ, that I dedicate this book. SDG.

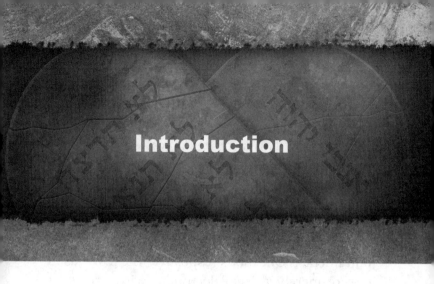

Introduction

Various events form a kaleidoscopic image in my mind about the Ten Commandments. I once observed a demonstration relating to a controversy over efforts to place the Decalogue in courthouses across the country. I wondered as I saw the protestors marching, *How many of these people have the Law read to them in their own churches during public worship?* I remember listening to a radio program in which the hosts interviewed a number of people during a Christian booksellers convention, asking them to list the Ten Commandments. No one could name them all.

Another time I saw a politician speak about the importance of placing the Ten Commandments in public schools. When asked to name the commandments, however, he could only come up with one. Another contribution to this mental collage are the discussions about the Law that I've had with Christians over the years. A number of people only understood the Law as a series of prohibitions, and others said that Christ had done away with the Law. This latter point was especially true regarding the fourth commandment and Sabbath observance.

I have read many books on the Law, whether for recreation or for sermon preparation, which rarely referred to Christ vis-à-vis the Ten Commandments. One book exposited the Law as if it were merely a legal document with principles that should be applied to our present day civil government. It seems that tumbleweed was more likely to blow across the pages than a reference to Christ. What accounts for these different responses to the Law?

At one level we can say sloth accounts for the ignorance that too many in the church have regarding the Decalogue. We can remember sports statistics, e-mail addresses, phone numbers, birthdays, and the like, but have trouble naming what the Jews have called the Ten Words. Another contributing factor to this ignorance is that people believe they can extract the Law from the Bible with little attention to its historical or covenantal context. For example, some have tried to place stone monuments of the Ten Commandments in courthouses that do not carry its prologue, thereby bypassing questions such as: What is the historical context in which the Law was given? To whom was it given? Why was it given? Who gave it? Divorced from these all-important contextual questions, the Law is shorn from its biblical moorings and becomes a wax nose, pliable to a number of different political causes. Many well-intending Christians claim they have no religious agenda but merely want to return this country to its historic Judeo-Christian ethical roots. However, severing the Law from its historical context (that it was given to the people of Israel) and its covenantal context (YHWH, the God of Abraham, Isaac, and Jacob, who delivered Israel from Egypt) fails to recognize that the Law is far more than a memorial to a Judeo-Christian ethic. We must recognize with Paul that Christ is the fulfillment of the law (Rom. 10:4).

Far too many people look at the Law apart from Christ. They go from the Ten Commandments straight to its application to life, never asking the question: What about Christ? That inevitably leads to legalism, or the belief that we are able to fulfill the Law. Yet Paul says about this approach to the Law, "The sting of death is sin; and the strength of sin is the law" (1 Cor. 15:56). The Law is powerless to save—it only condemns. Therefore, Christians must look at the Law and ask how it relates to Christ. How has Christ fulfilled the Law? How has He removed its curse? How has He written it upon our hearts? Only Christ can remove the Law's condemnation and make it a friend. As Romans 8:1–4 says, "There is therefore now no condemnation to them which are in Christ Jesus, who walk not after the flesh, but after the Spirit. For the law of the Spirit of life in Christ Jesus hath made me free from the law of sin and death. For what the law could not do, in that it was weak through the flesh, God sending his own Son in the likeness of sinful flesh, and for sin, condemned sin in the flesh: that the righteousness of the law might be fulfilled in us, who walk not after the flesh, but after the Spirit."

The following diagram illustrates this important relationship between the Christian and the Law:

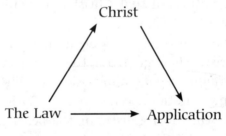

Moralism / Legalism

In studying the Law, we must first investigate it in its original historical setting: God giving the Law at Sinai. Second, we should see how God's covenantal dealings relate to the Law. That will help us recognize that God delivered His people from Egypt because of His covenant with Abraham, Isaac, and Jacob, then how Christ fulfilled the

Abrahamic covenant. Third, we must consider the redemptive context of the Law and determine how Christ fulfilled the Law. We must recognize that we are participants, not in the Mosaic covenant, but in the new covenant through Christ's shed blood. Keeping these three contexts in mind, we will see how the Law points to Christ and how He applies it to us by the indwelling power and presence of the Holy Spirit. In this light, our prayer should be that the church will increase its understanding of how the Law points to Christ and our need for redemption as well as to the holiness that should characterize those who are in union with Jesus.

Before moving on to our treatment of the Ten Commandments, we should take note of one more important aspect of the Law. The Law is not merely a legal bond; it is also the rule of love between God and His people. Recall the first and greatest commandment: "And thou shalt love the LORD thy God with all thine heart, and with all thy soul, and with all thy might" (Deut. 6:5). This same emphasis can be found in Christ's teaching to the church: "If ye love me, keep my commandments" (John 14:15). Hence, we must see that breaking God's Law is violating that bond of love. Alternatively, Christ fulfilled that rule of love because He loved His Father, obeying Him perfectly (John 17:4). And now, the Holy Spirit applies the Word to us and enables us to love our triune God, to obey our heavenly Father. To this end the apostle

John writes, "By this we know that we love the children of God, when we love God, and keep his commandments. For this is the love of God, that we keep his commandments: and his commandments are not grievous" (1 John 5:2–3). Hence the Law is a rule of love, one broken by Israel, fulfilled by Christ, and applied by the Spirit.

To gain an appropriate understanding of the Law, it is crucial to study the prologue to the Ten Commandments. It is therefore to the prologue that we turn.

STUDY QUESTIONS

1. How important is it to consider Christ in relation to the Ten Commandments?

2. Have you witnessed the legalistic results of failing to relate Christ to the Law?

3. What does it mean to consider the Law in its historical, covenantal, and redemptive contexts?

4. What are some ways that God's love relates to the Law?

5. In what ways does the Law reflect the level of love in our hearts?

The Prologue

The Ten Commandments is one of the best-known passages in the Bible. While unbelievers might have difficulty finding the Ten Commandments in Scripture, they and believers can give some account of what the Decalogue includes. Familiarity with the Decalogue has its benefits, since people do not need to struggle to understand the subject matter. Familiarity, on the other hand, has its drawbacks, since people tend to ignore what they believe they understand. For example, public displays of the Ten Commandments, whether in the church or in the public square, often omit the prologue (Ex. 20:1–2). Why are the first two verses of the Ten Commandments important? Let us see how necessary the prologue is to the proper understanding of the Ten Commandments.

The Prologue

In Exodus 20 God precedes the giving of the Law with these words: "And God spake all these words, saying" (Ex. 20:1). While these words might not strike us as significant, they are, for they clearly indicate the divine origin of the Law. The Decalogue was not just written by God; it is the very Word of God. While subsequent Scripture attributes the authorship of the Law to Moses (Ex. 24:4; John 1:45), its prologue tells us that the ultimate author is God.

Moving forward, we read: "I am the LORD thy God, which have brought thee out of the land of Egypt, out of the house of bondage" (Ex. 20:2). Notice that God prefaces the Law with two important facts: (1) YHWH is their God, and (2) He is the one who has redeemed Israel from slavery in Egypt. These two elements are key because this first places the Law within God's covenantal dealings with Israel. Remember, the one true God, creator of heaven and earth, revealed Himself to Moses and demonstrated His power in the ten plagues that He sent against Egypt. At the same time, God delivered Israel from Egypt because of the covenant promise He had made to Abraham. As Exodus 2:24 says: "And God heard their groaning, and God remembered his covenant with Abraham, with Isaac, and with Jacob." God delivered Israel from Egypt because of His covenant with Abraham. That offers us a multifaceted context from which to view the Law. In the realm of God's covenant with Abraham and His gracious dealings with His people, God has already saved Israel from slavery in Egypt. So the Law is not revealed to God's people as the means by which they should earn their redemption. Rather, the Law is revealed to show them how they can be conformed to the image of their loving, covenant Lord.

We know that Israel was to be conformed to the image of her covenant Lord because God called Israel to be a kingdom of priests and a holy nation (Ex. 19:5–6). The Law was the tool to show Israel what it meant to be a holy nation as well as to reveal God's character and attributes. The Law was not revealed so that Israel could earn redemption. Rather, Israel was to continuously remember her redeemed state in her reflection upon the Law. That is evident from God's own instructions to Israel:

> And when thy son asketh thee in time to come, saying, What mean the testimonies, and the statutes, and the judgments, which the LORD our God hath commanded you? Then thou shalt say unto thy son, We were Pharaoh's bondmen in Egypt; and the LORD brought us out of Egypt with a mighty hand: and the LORD shewed signs and wonders, great and sore, upon Egypt, upon Pharaoh, and upon all his household, before our eyes: and he brought us out from thence, that he

might bring us in, to give us the land which
he sware unto our fathers (Deut. 6:20–23).

Notice the interpretive instructions here: when
the children ask about the significance of the Law,
the first part of the answer is how God, the creator of heaven and earth, has redeemed them
from slavery in Egypt. Moreover, Israel's redemption was the fulfillment of the covenant promise
to bring them to the land of promise, which God
swore by a covenant to give to Abraham, Isaac,
and Jacob. This information is crucial when we
consider the relevance of the Ten Commandments
for the church today.

The Prologue Today

We must always read the prologue along with
the Ten Commandments because it sets the Law
within its historical, covenantal, and redemptive
contexts. In searching for the significance of the
Ten Commandments for the church today, we
must likewise consider the Law within our own
historical, covenantal, and redemptive contexts.

Our Historical Context

We do not stand at the foot of Mt. Sinai today and
receive the Law as Israel did in the Old Testament.
We stand at a point in time after the life, death,
and resurrection of our Lord and Savior, Jesus
Christ. The advent of Christ is crucial for under-

standing the Law for the church today, for we must interpret the Law in the light of the revelation of Christ. Historically, then, we must account for the person and work of Christ.

Our Covenantal Context

Like Israel, we must also consider our covenantal context. We are not the recipients of the Mosaic covenant, as Israel was, but instead are the recipients of the fulfillment of the Abrahamic and Mosaic covenants. In other words, with the revelation of the life, death, and resurrection of Christ, redemptive history has taken great steps forward. This means first, we must recognize that we receive the fulfillment of the Abrahamic covenant, the ground of the Mosaic covenant, with the revelation of Christ. The apostle Paul, commenting on the Abrahamic covenant (Gen. 12:7), explains: "Now to Abraham and his seed were the promises made. He saith not, And to seeds, as of many; but as of one, and to thy seed, which is Christ" (Gal. 3:16). In other words, receiving the Law was not the culmination of redemptive history. Rather, the Abrahamic covenant looked beyond the Mosaic covenant to its fulfillment in the advent of Christ.

Second, we no longer live under the economy of the Mosaic covenant but under the economy of the new covenant, ratified by the blood of Christ. As Hebrews 8:6–7 says: "But now hath he obtained a more excellent ministry, by how much also he is the mediator of a better covenant, which was established upon better promises. For if that first covenant had been faultless, then should no place have been sought for the second" (cf. 12:24). Our covenantal context, therefore, is not the Mosaic covenant but the new covenant mediated by Jesus Christ.

Our Redemptive Context

Just as Israel was to recall its redemptive context, namely, its deliverance from bondage in Egypt (Deut. 6:20–23), so we must continually remember our own redemptive context. We must remember that the events of the Old Testament foreshadowed the events of the New Testament. For example, the Passover (Exodus 12) foreshadowed the sacrifice of the true Passover Lamb, Jesus Christ: "For even Christ our passover is sacrificed for us" (1 Cor. 5:7). In this regard, Israel's deliverance foreshadowed our own deliverance. Israel was in bondage to Pharaoh, and we were in bondage to Satan, sin, and death. God "hath delivered us from the power of darkness, and hath translated us into the kingdom of his dear Son: in whom we have redemption through his blood, even the forgiveness of sins" (Col. 1:13–14). In this light, we might state the prologue for today as: "I am the LORD your God, who brought you out of slavery to Satan, sin, and death, by the life, death, and resurrection of Christ."

There are more parallels between Israel and the church. Recall that Israel was supposed to be a kingdom of priests and a holy nation (Ex. 19:5–6). If the Old Testament foreshadowed New Testament events and realities, we should not be surprised that the apostle Peter gave the New Testament church the same calling as Old Testament Israel: "Ye are a chosen generation, a royal priesthood, an holy nation, a peculiar people; that ye should shew forth the praises of him who hath called you out of darkness into his marvelous light" (1 Pet. 2:9).

In remembering our historical, covenantal, and redemptive contexts, we cannot examine the Law and its significance for the church apart from Christ. For we stand after the work of Christ in the new covenant mediated by Him, redeemed out of the kingdom of darkness. The Law is therefore not the means of our redemption, just as it was not for Israel.

The Purpose of the Law

The Law was never intended to be the means for earning our salvation. On the contrary, since the Abrahamic covenant was fulfilled in Christ, the same promise upon which Israel's redemption from Egypt was founded, then it stands to reason that the Israelites were to look to Christ, not the Law, for their redemption. Note how Paul explains the purpose of the Law: "For if the inheritance be of the law, it is no more of promise: but God gave

it to Abraham by promise. Wherefore then serveth
the law? It was added because of transgressions,
till the seed should come to whom the promise was
made" (Gal. 3:18–19b). Paul goes on to say, "But
before faith came, we were kept under the law,
shut up unto the faith which should afterwards
be revealed. Wherefore the law was our schoolmaster to bring us unto Christ, that we might be
justified by faith" (Gal. 3:23–24).

The Israelites were to look at the Law, see that
they did not measure up to its rigorous demands,
then look to the only one who could fulfill the
requirements of the Law—Jesus Christ. Again,
Paul writes:

> And the law is not of faith: but, The man
> that doeth them shall live in them. Christ
> hath redeemed us from the curse of the law,
> being made a curse for us: for it is written,
> Cursed is every one that hangeth on a tree:
> that the blessing of Abraham might come
> on the Gentiles through Jesus Christ; that
> we might receive the promise of the Spirit
> through faith (Gal. 3:12–14).

The Law is not the agent of our salvation—
it is not a stepladder by which we can climb the
heights of Mt. Zion and earn God's favor by our
obedience to the Law. No. The Law was revealed
to show us our inability to fulfill its requirements
and to bring a curse against us so that in despera-

tion we would cry out to Christ, the only one who can fulfill the requirements of the Law. Indeed, as Paul says, Christ suffered the penalty of the Law by becoming a curse for us.

The Implications of a Christ-centered Approach to the Law

I hope it is now evident why we must never separate the Ten Commandments from its prologue (Ex. 20:1–2). The prologue reminded Israel of her gracious redemption and directed her to the coming redemption of Christ. If we separate the Ten Commandments from its historical, covenantal, and redemptive contexts, we are left with a document that is neither Jewish nor Christian. Can we then post the Ten Commandments without its prologue in public places, courthouses, government buildings, and schools?

When people read, "Thou shalt have no other gods before me" (Ex. 20:3), they might ask in some confusion: To whom does this statement refer? Who is speaking? What is the context? What god has made this demand? Divorced from the prologue, the Ten Commandments are disconnected from their historical (the Law delivered at Sinai), covenantal (the fulfillment of the Abrahamic covenant), and redemptive contexts (the deliverance from Egypt). By disconnecting the Law from its moorings, the Law becomes the very thing it was never intended to be, a legalistic ladder by which some might attempt to earn salvation. When the prologue is connected to the Law, it ultimately directs us to Christ, for it points us to the Abrahamic covenant, which finds its fulfillment in Christ. Jesus has fulfilled the bond of love on our behalf.

Does the Law Only Function as a Guardian?

Let us consider one last question before we explore the commandments themselves. Does the Law function merely as a schoolmaster or guardian to drive us to Christ (Gal. 3:18–26)? In other words, does the Law have any other function?

Many people believe the Law only has the negative function of pointing out our sin. However, the Law also has a positive function. Paul writes, for example, "Wherefore the law is holy, and the commandment holy, and just, and good" (Rom. 7:12). In a similar way James writes: "If ye fulfill the royal law according to the scripture, Thou shalt love thy neighbour as thyself, ye do well" (James 2:8). Based upon such passages of Scripture, the Reformed church teaches there are three functions of the Law: (1) political—to restrain evil in the public realm; (2) pedagogical—the guardian aspect of which Paul speaks, which drives us to Christ; and (3) normative—the Law no longer condemns the believer because of the work of Christ but is now a guide for Christian behavior (cf. WCF 19.6).

According to Exodus 19:5–6, Israel was to be

a kingdom of priests and a holy nation. She was to shine forth the image of her Creator before the world. As Israel foreshadowed the church, we, too, have been called to be a kingdom of priests and a holy nation to shine forth the image of our Lord and Savior, Jesus Christ, before the world. Thus, when we read the Law, we must always be mindful of our redemption through Christ. At the same time we must realize that we are reading about the image and perfect righteousness of Jesus Christ. Christ perfectly fulfilled the obligations of the Law. If we are to reflect the image of Christ, the Law will assist us by showing us what we are supposed to look like. With the psalmist, we should love the Law of God because it shows us who we are in Christ and the righteousness with which we are to shine forth. As we examine the Law, we cannot simply explore ethical questions, for to do so is to divorce the Law from the prologue. Rather, we are to remember the trajectory that the prologue sets and which terminates in Christ. We must always examine the Law in connection with Christ.

Conclusion

The Law of God is good, but it will only be good for us if we use it the way God intended. We must read the Law in its historical, covenantal, and redemptive contexts so that our gaze will inevitably fall upon Christ. As we read the Law, may it reveal our sinfulness and wickedness, remind us of our need for redemption, and drive us to Christ. May we remember that we need not fear the condemnation of the Law because Christ has become a curse for us and has borne the curse of the Law upon the cross. May we also love the Law of God as it points us to the perfect righteousness of Jesus Christ, in whose image we are being renewed. Let us therefore give thanks for the Law of God and for Jesus Christ, who has fulfilled the Law on our behalf. May we never divorce the Law from its prologue, for to do so is to divorce it from Christ.

STUDY QUESTIONS

1. Why is the prologue important for the comprehension of the Ten Commandments as a whole?

2. Why must we account for the original historical context of the giving of the Law?

3. What difference does the ministry of Christ make for how we approach the Law?

4. In what way is the Law a guardian or schoolmaster that drives us to Christ?

5. How is the Law a guide for holy living?

The First Commandment

In approaching the Ten Commandments, we must first remember that any time we meditate upon the Law we must recall our redemption. This was the method that God gave to the Israelites: "And when thy son asketh thee in time to come, saying, What mean the testimonies, and the statutes, and the judgments, which the LORD our God hath commanded you? Then thou shalt say unto thy son, We were Pharaoh's bondmen in Egypt; and the LORD brought us out of Egypt with a mighty hand" (Deut. 6:20–21).

Today, we do not stand at the foot of Sinai to receive the Law. Rather, we live after the advent of Jesus Christ, "who hath delivered us from the power of darkness, and hath translated us into the kingdom of his dear Son: in whom we have redemption through his blood, even the forgiveness of sins" (Col. 1:13–14). Jesus Christ fulfilled the covenant promises that were given to Abraham and were the basis for Israel's deliverance from Egypt and the Mosaic covenant. As Galatians 3:16 says, "Now to Abraham and his seed were the promises made. He saith not, And to seeds, as of many; but as of one, and to thy seed, which is Christ." Keeping our historical, covenantal, and redemptive contexts in mind, let us examine the first commandment, which deals with the exclusive worship of the one true God.

In Its Original Setting

The first commandment says, "Thou shalt have no other gods before me" (Ex. 20:3). When we see this commandment within its historic setting, we begin to appreciate its significance. Also, when we consider this commandment in connection with the prologue, these words make sense: "I am the LORD thy God, which have brought thee out of the land of Egypt, out of the house of bondage" (Ex. 20:2). The Israelites saw God, YHWH, deliver them from Egypt. God brought about their redemption by judging the gods of Egypt. He said in Exodus 12:12: "I will pass through the land of Egypt this night, and will smite all the firstborn in the land of Egypt, both man and beast; and against all the gods of Egypt I will execute judgment: I am the LORD." If we examine the plagues that God sent upon Egypt, we soon realize that many of them represented God's sovereignty over Egyptian deities.

For example, turning the waters of the Nile into blood plunged a dagger into the heart of the god of the Nile (Ex. 7:14–25). The plague of frogs declared that Yʜᴡʜ was sovereign, not Heket, the frog goddess of childbirth (Ex. 8:1–15). God struck down the livestock of Egypt to show that Hathor, the sky goddess depicted as a cow, had no power over God (Ex. 9:1–7). And when God sent darkness upon the land, it taunted Pharaoh, who was supposed to be the incarnation of the sun god, Re (Ex. 10:21–29). The plagues against Egypt proved that the God of Israel was the one true God, for He alone was able to deliver Israel from Egypt, Pharaoh, and the Egyptian gods. The supremacy of God over all other gods is also evident in other passages of the Old Testament.

When we consider that Genesis 1–3 was most likely written about the time of Israel's exodus from Egypt, we realize that not only was God sovereign over the Egyptian pantheon but that He alone was the creator of heaven and earth. The Israelites were not to worship creation, trees, mountains, or oceans, for God had created them all. The Israelites were not to worship animals, for God had created them all. The Israelites were not to worship the sun, moon, stars, or planets, because God had created them. God tells Israel they are to have no other gods: "That they may know from the rising of the sun, and from the west, that there is none beside me. I am the Lᴏʀᴅ, and there is none else" (Isa. 45:6; cf. 45:21). Israel was to have no other gods, because Y<small>HWH</small> was the one and only true God.

This first commandment not only told Israel who God was but also what He had done for them. God had redeemed Israel as His bride from the house of bondage in Egypt. Y<small>HWH</small> appears as husband and Israel as bride throughout the Old Testament. Something of this marital intimacy is evident in the the first commandment where the Hebrew literally says, "You shall have no other gods before My face." No other nation on the earth enjoyed being in the presence of God—only Israel, who carried the tabernacle, the very house of God, which was pitched in her midst. Israel was to worship God, and Him alone, not only because He was the only true God but because He was in a special and unique relationship with Israel, which the Old Testament describes as a marriage (cf. Hos. 2:2). As we often hear in traditional marriage vows, when a couple marries, they promise to forsake all others. That was the kind of devotion Israel was expected to give in covenant to the Lord. It is reflected in the Shema of Israel: "Hear, O Israel: The L<small>ORD</small> our God is one L<small>ORD</small>: and thou shalt love the L<small>ORD</small> thy God with all thine heart, and with all thy soul, and with all thy might" (Deut. 6:4–5). God loved Israel and expected her to love Him back. But as we all know, Israel broke the bond of love that God had made with her.

In the Light of Christ

When we consider the Ten Commandments, we must do so remembering that we do not stand at the foot of Mt. Sinai but rather after the life, death, and resurrection of Christ. Moreover, when we look into the law of God, we behold more than God's character and attributes. We also see the perfect righteousness of Jesus Christ. This point is reflected in the opening verses of the book of Hebrews: "God, who at sundry times and in divers manners spake in time past unto the fathers by the prophets, hath in these last days spoken unto us by his Son" (Heb. 1:1–2a). In other words, the commandment to have no other gods before YHWH also teaches us that we are to have no other gods before our triune Lord who is supremely revealed in Jesus Christ. The themes of redemption and the exclusivity of the worship of our triune Lord through Christ alone is emphasized in Christ's famous statement: "I am the way, the truth, and the life: no man cometh unto the Father, but by me" (John 14:6). We may note, as C. S. Lewis once said, that there are only three interpretive options for this statement of Christ: He is a liar, on the level of a demon; He is a lunatic, on the level of one who considers himself a poached egg; or He is truly the Lord, and our obligation is to worship Him as such. Further connections between the revelation of God in Jesus Christ are recorded in other parts of the New Testament.

The Book of Acts states, "And it shall come to pass, that whosoever shall call on the name of the Lord shall be saved" (Acts 2:21). Here Peter is quoting Joel 2:32, which in its original context says that "whosoever shall call on the name of the LORD shall be delivered." Peter now clarifies that, saying that to call upon the name of YHWH is to call upon the name of Christ: "This is the stone which was set at nought of you builders, which is become the head of the corner. Neither is there salvation in any other: for there is none other name under heaven given among men, whereby we must be saved" (Acts 4:11–12). Thus we, too, must recognize that we owe allegiance and worship to our triune Lord, who is supremely revealed in Jesus Christ. For just as God declared His supremacy over false deities in delivering Israel from Egypt, so the Lord Jesus Christ "is over all, God blessed for ever" (Rom. 9:5). Moreover, as Israel was to worship God alone because she was His wife, so we too must remember that Christ is our husband and we, the church, are His bride (Eph. 5:25–30). When Christ delivers us out of the kingdom of darkness into the kingdom of light, we are joined to Him by faith to forsake all others and to worship Him, and Him alone.

As we reflect upon the first commandment in the light of Christ, we may think that we are not prone to such silly idolatrous behavior as the worship of cows or frogs. We may think we are far

more sophisticated than our Old Testament coun-
terparts; we no longer believe in such antiquated
notions. Yet, despite our modern advancements, we
are still as idolatrous as ever and worship all sorts
of things. Paul makes that clear in the first chapter of Romans: "Professing themselves to be wise,
they became fools, and changed the glory of the
uncorruptible God into an image made like to corruptible man, and to birds, and fourfooted beasts,
and creeping things" (Rom. 1:22–23). Indeed, how
often do we refuse to acknowledge the existence
of any god, yet check our horoscope in the local
paper or read the messages in fortune cookies? The
worship of false gods abounds in every age, which
is why the apostle John closes his first epistle with
the words: "Little children, keep yourselves from
idols" (1 John 5:21). All people have the obligation
to believe in the one true God as He is revealed in
Jesus Christ. With the apostles, we must say that
there is no other name under heaven or earth by
which we can be saved.

The Connection to the Church

In examining the first commandment, we see
the second use of the law, namely, the command
to worship God only and to have no other gods
before Him. When the Holy Spirit applies this
commandment to the heart of the unbeliever in
regeneration or even the regenerate believer, He
causes the person to flee to Christ. Moreover, the

Spirit enables us to love the triune God and in this way applies the rule of love to our hearts. We hear the demands of the Law, recognize our sin in worshiping other gods, and flee to Christ, the revelation of the one true God. We then recognize the third use of the Law, namely, that the Law is a guide to us for holy living (see Westminster Confession of Faith 19.6). We must therefore constantly meditate upon the first commandment and ask ourselves: Do we worship any other gods besides the one true God as He is revealed in Christ? We might initially say no, yet, if we truly consider what idolatry consists of, perhaps we might reconsider whether we obey the first commandment to its fullest.

The Heidelberg Catechism defines idolatry, saying: "It is, instead of the one true God who has revealed himself in his Word, or along with the same, to conceive or have something else on which to place our trust" (Q. 95). Therefore, any time we put something or someone in place of our triune Lord, we violate the first commandment. To illustrate, consider that Scripture says man's strength can be his god (Hab. 1:11). Possessions can be a god (Job 31:24). Wealth can be a god (Matt. 6:24). We can even make food a god (Phil. 3:19). And family can be a god (Matt. 10:37–38). We can easily turn anything into an idol by placing our trust in that rather than in our triune Lord. Allow me to further illustrate this point.

How many Christians move to a city because their company has transferred them there, and only after they have moved discover there is not a good church in the area? How much better it would be if Christians examined the area prior to a move, then told their employers, "No, I cannot accept this new job and an increased salary because there is not a solid church at which my family and I can worship." How can a Christian claim to love Christ, yet place a job over his worship of Christ? If Christ is truly our chief concern in this life, the one whom we truly love with all our heart, then we must be willing to say no to anything in this world that could take the place of Christ.

We see the righteousness of Christ with respect to the first commandment in His unwillingness to bow the knee to worship Satan. As Matthew 4:9–10 tells us, Jesus responded to Satan's promise to give Him all the things of the world if He would just bow to Satan and worship him by saying, "Get thee hence, Satan: for it is written, Thou shalt worship the Lord thy God, and him only shalt thou serve." We also see Christ's obedience to the first commandment in the garden of Gethsemane when He says, "O my Father, if this cup may not pass away from me, except I drink it, thy will be done" (Matt. 26:42). Paul also describes Christ's submission to His Father's will in Philippians 2:5–11, saying Christ was willing to be obedient even unto death rather than to seek His own will. Christ fulfilled the bond of love and was obedient to His Father; nothing interfered with the supreme place of His Father's will in His life. So, too, nothing must interfere with the supreme place of our triune Lord as revealed in Jesus Christ. Jobs, family, money, possessions, or desires, must never supplant the supreme position of Christ as Lord in our hearts.

Conclusion

When we study the first commandment, we must always do so in the light of our redemption in Christ. We should reflect upon the first commandment and allow it to roam freely in our hearts, bringing its demands for perfect love to God to bear against our sinful and idolatrous desires. We must then flee to Christ, knowing that in His incarnation is the fulfillment of every aspect of the law, for He refused to bow to Satan and was obedient to the will of His heavenly Father. Christ worshiped no other gods.

At the same time, we should reflect upon the law as believers so that we may see Jesus Christ, in whose image we are being renewed on a daily basis. The Law must constantly remind us that idolatry is incompatible with who we are in Christ. We can then rejoice in the knowledge that when Christ returns, we will have every idolatrous desire removed from our hearts and wills, as the greatest commandment states, love the Lord our God with all our hearts, souls, and minds (Matt. 22:37). The first commandment can thus be summarized: we must love our heavenly Father, for He has sent His Son to redeem us from the bondage of sin and death; therefore, we must forsake all others.

STUDY QUESTIONS

1. What were the different Egyptian "gods" that the one true God judged in the plagues against Egypt?

2. In what way does Genesis 1–3 inform the historical context of the giving of the Law as it pertains to the first commandment?

3. What does the first commandment expect of God's people?

4. What does the Heidelberg Catechism explain as a false god?

5. In what way did Christ fulfill the first commandment?

The Second Commandment

John Calvin once said people are a perpetual idol factory. The second commandment addresses issues related to idol-making, specifically carved images. Many people say this commandment only refers to making carved or pictographic images of the Godhead. True enough, all images of the Godhead are prohibited. Nevertheless, when we consider this commandment in the light of Christ, we find that far greater redemptive truths are taught in the second commandment—truths that are revealed in Christ and that bring tremendous blessing upon the believer. Before we proceed, though, let us remember the historical, covenantal, and redemptive contexts of this commandment (Deut. 6:20–21; Col. 1:13–14; Gal. 3:16).

In Its Original Setting

The second commandment says, "Thou shalt not

make unto thee any graven image, or any likeness
of any thing that is in heaven above, or that is in
the earth beneath, or that is in the water under the
earth" (Ex. 20:4). As we saw in the first commandment, we are to worship God and God alone. Idols of
any sort are not permitted. The second commandment gives the Israelites instructions regarding the
manner in which God is to be worshiped. It says
the Israelites were not to make any carved images
for the purpose of worship. They could not make
carved images of other so-called deities, but they
also could not make any carved images of Yhwh,
the one true God, to facilitate their worship of Him.
The Israelites were not to use images of anything
in creation to visualize Yhwh.

The second commandment goes on to say:
"Thou shalt not bow down thyself to them, nor
serve them: for I the Lord thy God am a jealous
God, visiting the iniquity of the fathers upon the
children unto the third and fourth generation
of them that hate me; and shewing mercy unto
thousands of them that love me, and keep my
commandments" (Ex. 20:5–6). This explicit prohibition of worshiping or serving carved images
is grounded in the jealousy of God. Jealousy is an
attribute of God that receives little attention but
is well attested to in Scripture. As Exodus 34:14
says, "For thou shalt worship no other god: for
the Lord, whose name is Jealous, is a jealous God."
Remember, though, that God's jealousy is governed

by holiness, not sin (cf. Isa. 6:3). God's jealousy is analogous to a husband or wife's desire that his or her spouse must forsake all others when joined in the covenant of marriage. God was Israel's husband; therefore she was to worship Him as He desired as well as to dispense with images of other gods. As Jehovah's bride, Israel was to forsake all others and worship God alone.

In some respects, the second commandment is unique in naming threats as well as blessings. If Israel disobeyed this commandment, God would visit the consequences of her sin upon her children to the third and fourth generations, the commandment says. Note that God visits the consequences of sins of the fathers upon the children of those who *hate* Him. By contrast, God visits His blessings upon, literally, "thousands," which implies a multitude of generations, of those who love him. This blessing-curse aspect of the commandment is unique in its appended stipulation; however, such a stipulation is inherent not only in this commandment but in all of the commandments.

Can we really say that an Israelite could violate the first commandment, for example, with no ill effects for future generations? No. At the same time, we must recognize that this appended condition does not contradict other passages of Scripture such as Deuteronomy 24:16, which says, "The fathers shall not be put to death for the children, neither shall the children be put to death for the fathers: every man shall be put to death for his own sin." This verse from Deuteronomy specifically speaks about the sins of an individual and whether or not offspring are held accountable for that sin. Individual responsibility for sin is different from what is mentioned in the second commandment. The second commandment refers to the nation of Israel as a whole in its warning about the consequences of sin. If the nation of Israel fails to obey the second commandment, future generations will suffer as rebellion and disobedience beget more rebellion. Hence God's judgment falls upon future generations because they will also hate God. At the same time, we see God's mercy in the appended condition; namely, His love is poured upon thousands of generations, and even those whom He judges only suffer but for a time. The question naturally arises, however: Why did God prohibit Israel from making graven images of Him?

First, God prohibited the fabrication of images of Himself because He does not have a body. We read in John 4:24: "God is a spirit." Moses could not see God when he climbed to the top of Mt. Sinai. Hence, how can people reproduce what they cannot see? Second, God prohibited the making and worship of images because He wanted to maintain His sovereignty. God's desire to protect His sovereignty is evident in the golden-calf incident. Some believe making the golden calf was a violation of the first commandment; here, at the foot of Sinai, Israel worshiped another god. This misunderstanding is based upon the translation of the verse: "The people gathered themselves together unto Aaron, and said unto him, Up, make us gods, which shall go before us" (Ex. 32:1). The translation of *elohim* as "gods" is possible because it is the Hebrew word for gods, but *elohim* can also be translated as the generic noun for God. Given the context of this verse, a preferable translation is, "Up, make us God, YHWH." Notice that Aaron did not produce multiple gods but only one golden calf (Ex. 32:4). Israel wanted to see YHWH, so Aaron made an image to visualize the one true God who delivered them out of Egypt. The people were tired of waiting for Moses to come down from Sinai and thought they could summon God by creating an image of Him. They loved themselves more than their Lord and broke the bond of love. With this image they thought they could control God, move Him about, and worship Him when and where they pleased. Such insubordination in the hearts of men is why God did not want His people to make images of Him; God wanted His people to recognize that He was sovereign over them, not they over Him.

In the Light of Christ
The third reason for prohibiting graven images of God is that the right to create such images was the

exclusive right of God alone. Whatever image man might create would always fall short of accurately portraying God, which is certainly evident in the golden calf. Imagine using a cow to visualize the one true, living God when Israel knew that God had created the cow. God has exclusive rights to creating His own image. And it is a copyright that He will never surrender.

There has been one creature in all of the cosmos to whom God has given His image, and that is, of course, man: "So God created man in his own image, in the image of God created he him; male and female created he them" (Gen. 1:27). Man, in many ways, is the best reflection of God and His attributes, such as righteousness, holiness, the ability to create, the ability to relate to God, and His dominion over creation. But Adam and Eve rebelled against God, and though we as humans still bear the image of God, that image has been marred and obscured by sin. In a pristine world, unsullied by sin, people would have looked at each other and would have seen the reflection of the divine image, which then would have turned them to worship the one true God. As a result of the fall, however, man began worshiping his own image rather than God. That sin is no more clearly evident than in the sin of homosexuality. Romans 1 tells us:

> Professing themselves to be wise, they be-
> came fools, and changed the glory of the

uncorruptible God into an image made like to corruptible man, and to birds, and four-footed beasts, and creeping things.... For this cause God gave them up unto vile affections: for even their women did change the natural use into that which is against nature: and likewise also the men, leaving the natural use of the woman, burned in their lust one toward another; men with men working that which is unseemly, and receiving in themselves that recompense of their error which was meet (Rom. 1:22–23, 26–27).

When we reflect upon the image of God, we must ultimately look to Christ. As previously stated, when we gaze into the Law, we not only see the reflection of God's being and attributes, but we ultimately view the perfect righteousness of Jesus Christ. Christ's presence in the Law is especially evident in the second commandment.

Consider what Paul wrote regarding the first Adam: "Nevertheless death reigned from Adam to Moses, even over them that had not sinned after the similitude of Adam's transgression, who is the figure of him that was to come" (Rom. 5:14). Notice that Adam was a "figure of him that was to come," namely Jesus Christ. God will never surrender the copyright to His image because that image is ultimately fulfilled in Jesus Christ. Note what Christ said to His disciples concerning their desire to see God the Father: "Have I been so long time with you, and yet hast thou not known me? He that hath seen me hath seen the Father" (John 14:8–9b). God, who is spirit, is revealed in His Son, Jesus Christ. To see Christ, then, is to see the Father.

It is no wonder, then, that Scripture so often tells us that Jesus Christ is "the express image of his person" (Heb. 1:3). We read, "In whom the god of this world hath blinded the minds of them which believe not, lest the light of the glorious gospel of Christ, who is the image of God, should shine unto them" (2 Cor. 4:4). We cannot manufacture images of God because Jesus Christ has already taken that role. Only Christ can do what no man-made image can, namely, perfectly reflect the image of God. Moreover, unlike man-made images that were created so man might exercise his authority over God, Christ, the perfect image of God, was completely obedient to the will of His heavenly Father (Phil. 2:5–11). So, the reason that we must not worship God with any image is that we will inevitably fall short of the divine goal to worship God through Christ. Those who worship our triune Lord through the use of images violate the second commandment.

The Connection to the Church
God has made provision for our feeble and weak-minded thinking in wanting to see Him and

His Son. Moses wanted to see God and Thomas wanted to see Jesus. For the time being, God has depicted Christ in the sacraments—water, bread, and wine—which serve as a reminder that on the final day we will behold the face of God in the face of Christ. When we want to see Christ, we can therefore look upon the sacraments and look upon His broken body and blood, not upon a crucifix or portrait of Christ. Bread and wine as well as the water of baptism are the Christ-ordained images that God allows in our worship. Even those are temporary until the conclusion of all things.

Inevitably, when we do supplement the worship of the one true God with an unauthorized image, we end up like the Israelites—worshiping the image rather than God. What we should see, then, is that the second commandment helps us maintain the purity of worship. The prohibition of images helped God's people from pretending they had sovereignty over Him. It was a constant reminder that Israel was the creature and God was the Creator. The problem with Israel's worship of the golden calf was that Israel thought she could worship God at a time and place of her choosing rather than submit to God's will not only in worship but even in daily living. Thousands of years have come and gone since Israel's golden calf idolatry, but people still try to worship God in a manner of their own choosing, both within and outside of the church. In an age of *will worship*—a term the Puritans used to denote worship according to man's rather than God's desires—the second commandment is still relevant.

Notice how the Westminster Shorter Catechism explains the second commandment: "The second commandment requires the receiving, observing, and keeping pure and entire, all such religious worship and ordinances as God hath appointed in his word" (Q. 50). That means we must apply the second commandment every time we worship God according to His revealed will, according to the Word. It also means that every time we fail to maintain the purity of worship, we fail to obey the second commandment.

Conclusion

The second commandment, as with all of the Law, directs us to Christ. It warns us of sin, then drives us to Christ who, through His life, death, and resurrection has fulfilled the bond of love. It points us to Christ in reminding us that we must never make an image of God because God has revealed His image perfectly in our Lord Jesus Christ. It points us to Christ because, rather than making images of God, we see that we are being remade into God's image. God is recreating us, eliminating every vestige of sin. As 2 Corinthians 3:18 says: "But we all, with open face beholding as in a glass the glory of the Lord, are changed into the same image from glory to glory, even as by the Spirit of the Lord." We do not make images of God, for He is making images of Himself in us! In this way, Christ applies the rule of love to us by creating His holy image in us. When we read the second commandment, therefore, we should not see it merely as a prohibition, for it is also a reminder of Christ and our re-creation in His image. Let us therefore look to Christ, the only true image of God, and rejoice in our redemption.

STUDY QUESTIONS

1. In what way does the second commandment guard the purity of worship?

2. What is *will worship*?

3. Why does God retain His "copyright" over His image?

4. Who is the uncreated image of God?

5. Who bears the created image of God in both creation but especially in redemption?

The Third Commandment

William Shakespeare once wrote, "What's in a name? That which we call a rose by any other name would smell as sweet." Shakespeare was saying that names can be artificial and in the end do not have much significance. However, everyone might not agree with Shakespeare's assertion. A person's name is a most significant element of his identity. It distinguishes him from all other people. For those that bear family names, a name can tell a story of great tradition, love, or even heroism. God's name says much about who He is and what He has done for His covenant people. This is one reason why God's name is sacred to Him and must be sacred to those who worship Him. As we explore the third commandment, we will be mindful of its historic, covenantal, and redemptive contexts as well as the prologue and God's covenantal promise to Abraham and Israel's redemption from Egypt. We will also remember that we are the recipients of the blessings of the Abrahamic covenant and that we live after the life, death, and resurrection of Christ.

In Its Original Setting

The third commandment says: "Thou shalt not take the name of the LORD thy God in vain; for the LORD will not hold him guiltless that taketh his name in vain" (Ex. 20:7). Why is God so concerned about protecting His name? We must understand that in Scripture there is a close connection between a person's name and his character. This connection is especially evident with the name of God, YHWH. Consider how God revealed His name to Moses in the burning bush:

> God said unto Moses, I AM THAT I AM: and he said, Thus shalt thou say unto the children of Israel, I AM hath sent me unto you. And God said moreover unto Moses, Thus shalt thou say unto the children of Israel, The LORD God of your fathers, the God of Abraham, the God of Isaac, and the God of Jacob, hath sent me unto you: this is my name for ever, and this is my memorial unto all generations (Ex. 3:14–15).

Notice that God's name Y$_{HWH}$ is translated as "I am who I am," which God then reduces to "I am." It is important to see that God's name is identical with His being and attributes and that in this sense is identical with His eternal nature. God's attributes are reflected in other portions of Scripture such as "Grace be unto you, and peace, from him which is, and which was, and which is to come" (Rev. 1:4; cf. 1:8; 4:8). God's name Y$_{HWH}$ conveys the idea of His eternal existence, His being, and His attributes.

Note that God also connects His name with His redemptive acts, particularly in His covenant with the patriarchs Abraham, Isaac, and Jacob. God so identifies His name with His redemptive activity that He says, "This is my memorial unto all generations," that is, "Y$_{HWH}$, the God of Abraham, Isaac, and Jacob." So a close connection, if not outright identification, exists between God's being, attributes, redemptive activity, and His name. Something of this connection is stated in the Psalms: "O LORD our Lord, how excellent is thy name in all the earth" (8:1)! We also read, "Nevertheless he saved them for his name's sake, that he might make his mighty power to be known" (Ps. 106:8). Likewise, "Unto thee, O God, do we give thanks, unto thee do we give thanks: for that thy name is near thy wondrous works declare" (Ps. 75:1). These passages show that people in Israel were to revere the name of Y$_{HWH}$ because it was so intimately connected with God's being, attributes, and redemptive activity.

Rather than loosely tossing about God's name in casual conversation, the Israelites were to "give unto the LORD the glory due unto his name" (Ps. 29:2) and to "sing forth the honour of his name" (Ps. 66:2). Israel was to respect the sanctity of the name of God, for God would hold accountable any person who used His name flippantly or for less than godly purposes. God's name could also be misused in false prophecy, or ascribing a prophecy to the Lord that He did not utter (Deut. 18:22). The prophet who deceitfully used the name of the Lord to add legitimacy to his claims was taking the Lord's name in vain by dishonoring God and His gracious redemption.

The Israelites were redeemed, not so they could commit lies and deceit like other nations, but so they could reflect the character of their covenant Lord. The Israelites were also told they should not take the name of the Lord in vain by using it to bolster a false oath (Jer. 5:2; Lev. 19:12). The Israelites should not attach the name of God to anything that was contrary to His nature or contrary to His gracious redemption of Israel. Maintaining the sanctity of God's name was so important that God would hold any Israelite accountable who violated His name by sending a curse upon him: "I will bring it forth, saith the LORD of hosts, and it shall enter into the house of the thief, and into the house of him that sweareth falsely by my name: and it shall remain in the midst of his house, and shall consume it with the timber thereof and the stones thereof" (Zech. 5:4; cf. Lev. 24:10–16). To curse the name of God was to curse His very existence and to heap insults upon Israel's redemption and the covenant promises God made to Abraham, Isaac, and Jacob.

In the Light of Christ

As we consider the third commandment in the light of the revelation of Christ, we must remember that the Law reflects God's character and attributes as well as Christ's person and His perfect righteousness. It is vital that we recognize Christ's connection to the third commandment. To do this, we must, first, remember that God's name is connected with His redemptive activity. This was especially evident when God told Moses that He was forever to be known as the God of Abraham, Isaac, and Jacob. If Christ was to be the fulfillment of the covenant promises that God made to the patriarchs, then Christ would be the embodiment, the very incarnation, of the name of God. This is certainly no more evident than in our Savior's name. *Jesus* is the English transliteration of the Greek name *Iesus*, which is the Greek transliteration of the name *Yehoshua*, which literally means, "Yʜᴡʜ is salvation." The name *Yehoshua* is the English translation of the Old Testament name

Joshua. Quite literally, the name of the Savior is Joshua. Jesus, therefore, is the incarnation of God's name and the fulfillment of God's covenant promises to Abraham, Isaac, and Jacob.

Through the life, death, and resurrection of Christ, we are redeemed from the dominion of Satan, sin, and death, and brought into the kingdom of God under the dominion of the tri-une Lord. For this reason Paul says of Christ to the Philippians, "Wherefore God also hath highly exalted him, and given him a name which is above every name: that at the name of Jesus every knee should bow, of things in heaven, and things in earth, and things under the earth; and that every tongue should confess that Jesus Christ is Lord, to the glory of God the Father" (Phil. 2:9–11). Christ is the very incarnation of the name of God. In Him are the being and attributes of God, for He is the second person of the Trinity, who is very God of very God, and the fulfillment of God's saving purposes manifest in the flesh.

The connection between the name of God and the name of Christ is clear in Peter's sermon at Pentecost where he quotes Joel 2:32: "Whosoever shall call on the name of the Lord shall be saved." In its original context the verse says, "Whosoever shall call on the name of the LORD," or YHWH, "shall be delivered." Peter directs his listeners to Jesus Christ, saying that to call on the name of YHWH is to call on the name of Jesus, who is God incarnate. Paul makes this same connection in Romans 10:13–17. Thus, as the apostle John says, people must place their faith in the name of Christ: "And this is his commandment, That we should believe on the name of his Son Jesus Christ, and love one another, as he gave us commandment" (1 John 3:23).

The Connection to the Church

Because Christ has already died and risen, we cannot look at the third commandment merely in terms of God's name. So many people look at this commandment and think that it is only violated when someone uses the name of God (or a derivative of it) as a curse word. True, cursing violates the third commandment, but not for the reasons that most people think. Cursing violates the third commandment not simply because a person carelessly uses the name of God or Christ. Rather, cursing violates the commandment because the person who misuses the name of God reveals with his mouth the low esteem he has for God's name and everything for which it stands.

People forget that the one true God is the God of Abraham, Isaac, and Jacob and has revealed Himself and His redemptive purposes in His Son, Jesus Christ. They forget that Jesus, the incarnation of God's name and saving purposes, fulfilled every obligation of the rule of love, died a painful, ignominious death on behalf of sinners, and was raised for our justification. Instead, in violat-

ing the third commandment, the name of God as
it is manifested in Christ becomes common and
mundane, just another word in our vocabulary,
an epithet in a long string of foul curse words, or
the exclamation point for anger and impatience,
rather than the name at which every knee will
bow and which every tongue will confess. We
should be mindful, then, of the way in which we
use the name of God.

Our desire should be not simply to refrain
from the abuse of the name of God but also to
use the name of God positively. Our desire should
be to praise the name of God for the blessings in
our lives: our redemption in Christ as well as the
familial, material, and financial blessings that we
receive by His grace. This is especially true in worship, where we lift high the name of Christ and
offer our spiritual sacrifice of praise. What greater
application of the rule of love can there be than to
praise and love God for His mercy shown in Christ
by His Spirit? We also rightly use the name of God
when we take oaths and vows, whether in a court
of law to tell the truth, in religious vows such as
those of church membership or marriage, or in
other such commitments (Deut. 6:13; Isa. 19:21;
cf. WCF 21.5). At the same time, we should realize
the extensive scope of the third commandment.

We must not limit the application of the commandment to our speech alone; our conduct is

certainly involved. Paul gives a warning, for example, to Titus about the conduct of God's people:

> That the aged men be sober, grave, temperate, sound in faith, in charity, in patience. The aged women likewise, that they be in behaviour as becometh holiness, not false accusers, not given to much wine, teachers of good things; that they may teach the young women to be sober, to love their husbands, to love their children, to be discreet, chaste, keepers at home, good, obedient to their own husbands, that the word of God be not blasphemed (Titus 2:2–5).

Notice how Paul's pastoral instructions to Titus connect the conduct of God's people to respect for the Word of God. The conduct of the church should be upright so that the outside world does not revile the Word of God. In this vein, the apostle John writes: "Beloved, if God so loved us, we ought also to love one another" (1 John 4:11).

How many people in the church, which bears the name of Christ, violate the third commandment by allowing their misconduct to bring reproach upon the name of Christ? How many people take the name of Christ in vain by claiming to be Christians, yet in their conduct deny that affirmation? I know a professing Christian who was fired from his company because he had vast quantities of pornography on his company computer. The person who told me about this incident was disheartened because a number of people in the office remarked, "I thought he was a Christian!"

God's name is identical with His being, attributes, and redemptive activity. God's name is forever, YHWH, the God of Abraham, Isaac, and Jacob. His name becomes incarnate in the life, death, and resurrection of Christ, who has delivered us from the bondage of sin and death, and is the name that is above every name, at which every knee will bow and every tongue confess. If we truly understand this, we will yearn not only to revere the name of Christ in our speech but in all of our lives.

As we reflect upon the third commandment, we see how often we violate it. We violate it when we flippantly or carelessly use the name of God or Christ. We violate it when our conduct does not honor the name of Christ. But we can flee to Him only in the knowledge that He is the Law incarnate and that in the Law we see His perfect righteousness. We can flee to Christ knowing that He has fulfilled God's rule of love, even this third commandment, because He is the incarnation of God's name and our redemption and salvation in the flesh. We can look at the third commandment as a guide to holy living, knowing what is pleasing to the Lord in the proper use of His name. We should also realize that our loyalty to the name of Christ will cause the unbelieving world to despise and hate us: "If ye be reproached for the name of Christ, happy are ye; for the spirit of glory and of God resteth upon you" (1 Pet. 4:14).

Conclusion

As we reflect upon the third commandment, we should be mindful of our language, for as James 3:10 says: "Out of the same mouth proceedeth blessing and cursing." We should also plumb the depths of this third commandment, recognizing that it deals with matters that go far beyond our speech. Our prayer should be that God will conform our very lives to the image of Christ by His Spirit by applying the rule of love to us. Let us long for the day that His redemption will culminate in our glorification, when we will no longer violate the third commandment. Indeed, at the time when Christ returns, we will completely become what we have declared: that we bear the name of Christ in word and deed.

STUDY QUESTIONS

1. Of what significance is a person's name in the Bible?

2. How did God connect His name to His redemptive activity?

3. Who ultimately reveals and bears God's name?

4. In what ways do we as Christians, those who bear the name of Christ, violate the third commandment?

5. Does the third commandment merely address misusing the name of God?

The Fourth Commandment

Sabbath observance today is at an all-time low. For many people, what was once an entire day devoted to public and private exercises of worship has been reduced to one hour. Many people come to church once a week to do sixty minutes of worship, then go about the rest of the day like their neighbors, running errands, shopping, mowing the grass, or watching a ball game. This trend shows that though many Christians profess to honor the Ten Commandments, in practice they have excised the fourth commandment from the Law.

While attention to various sins might ebb and flow over the centuries, true appreciation and understanding of the fourth commandment is critically needed today. The church needs to refresh its understanding and appreciation of this commandment. As we explore the fourth commandment, we will do so with an eye to its historic, covenantal, and redemptive contexts. We will also explore this commandment with an eye to its fulfillment in Christ and its relationship to the church.

In Its Original Setting

The fourth commandment states:

> Remember the sabbath day, to keep it holy. Six days shalt thou labour, and do all thy work: but the seventh day is the sabbath of the LORD thy God: in it thou shalt not do any work, thou, nor thy son, nor thy daughter, thy manservant, nor thy maidservant, nor thy cattle, nor thy stranger that is within thy gates: for in six days the LORD made heaven and earth, the sea, and all that in them is, and rested the seventh day: wherefore the LORD blessed the sabbath day, and hallowed it (Ex. 20:8–11).

In one way or another, we see various parts of the church rejecting the fourth commandment today. Some church leaders say this commandment is no longer binding upon the church because it was meant only for Israel. Others say Christ has fulfilled this commandment so it is no longer binding upon the church. Christ has certainly fulfilled this commandment, but that does not mean we can sweep it away. Indeed, Christ has fulfilled the whole law, yet we do not believe the commandment against murder, for example, is no longer binding upon the church. So, then, how should we relate the work of Christ to the fourth commandment? Let us examine the commandment in its original setting.

In the Old Testament, God commanded Israel to set aside the seventh day of every week as the Sabbath. The people were to do all of their work on six days of the week, then dedicate the seventh to worship the Lord. Just as God created the heavens and earth in six days and then rested, so too Israel was to rest after six days of work. The Sabbath was a sign of God's creational labor. We read that the day was "a sign between me and the children of Israel forever: for in six days the LORD made heaven and earth, and on the seventh day he rested, and was refreshed" (Ex. 31:17). Not only were the Israelites to stop working, but those under their authority were also commanded to rest, for the command was: "Six days thou shalt do thy work, and on the seventh day thou shalt rest: that thine ox and thine ass may rest, and the son of thy handmaid, and the stranger, may be refreshed" (Ex. 23:12). The Sabbath was to be a day of rest from work but also a day dedicated to the worship of God. Let us look deeper into this commandment so that we might understand why Sabbath rest was included in the Ten Commandments.

The origin of the fourth commandment is in creation itself. The fourth commandment is rooted in Genesis 1–2, not in Exodus with the people of

Israel in the sands of the Sinai desert. What, then, is the significance of the Sabbath? Some would argue that the commandment simply imitates God's pattern of work and rest. That is certainly true, yet there are more profound reasons for reminding Israel of Sabbath rest.

In the Garden of Eden, Adam and Eve were given the dominion mandate to multiply the image of God throughout the earth. They were to produce offspring in God's image and to spread the garden, the first temple, to the ends of the earth. Each Sabbath, Adam was to cease his labors to rest and contemplate the goodness of God. He was to worship God, meditate upon the completed goals of his labor, and experience a taste of God's rest. In other words, Adam was to contemplate and taste the eschatological goal of the creation, just as God did on the seventh day of creation. Later, God would ask Israel to recall the work of Adam and the rest of God that Adam failed to enter. Sabbath rest in the garden was an attainable goal for Adam, but Adam chose not to fulfill the dominion mandate but instead disobeyed the commandment of God.

Sabbath rest for Israel was a bit different. The Sabbath for Israel still represented the rest of God, the eternal rest that God entered on the seventh day of the creation week. In essence, God republished at Sinai the work principle that He first gave to Adam in the garden. Israel, however, would not enter God's rest by her labors, as Adam could have, but only by God's grace. Such grace is evident in how God characterizes the Sabbath: "Verily my sabbaths ye shall keep: for it is a sign between me and you throughout your generations; that ye may know that I am the Lord that doth sanctify you" (Ex. 31:13). Notice that God calls the Sabbath a sign, which means that it was a sign of the Mosaic covenant. In this, we should note two things.

First, the Sabbath was a sign that God dwelled among the Israelites, sanctifying them—in other words, setting them apart. He set them apart by freeing them from slavery in Egypt. Second, the penalty for working on the Sabbath was death: "Every one that defileth it shall surely be put to death: for whosoever doeth any work therein, that soul shall be cut off from among his people" (Ex. 31:14). When we understand the significance of the Sabbath, we realize that this penalty of death is not too harsh. If we read Deuteronomy's version of the fourth commandment, we see why labor was prohibited: "And remember that thou wast a servant in the land of Egypt, and that the Lord thy God brought thee out thence through a mighty hand and by a stretched out arm: therefore the Lord thy God commanded thee to keep the sabbath day" (Deut. 5:15). God anchors one reason for Sabbath rest, not in creation, but in the Israelites' deliverance from Egypt. The Israelites were to rest from their labors and to give all of those around them rest because God had delivered them from bondage. Israel was not freed from Egypt by her works but by the grace of God.

The Sabbath, then, was not only a day of rest, a cessation of labor, and a day to worship God, but it was also a day to celebrate Israel's redemption from slavery in Egypt. The reason God appended the death penalty to the fourth commandment is because Israel could not enter God's Sabbath rest by her own efforts but by God's grace. The fourth commandment, then, is a living portrait of Romans 6:23: "For the wages of sin is death; but the gift of God is eternal life through Jesus Christ our Lord." In other words, a person who worked on the Sabbath was telling the world that he could enter God's rest by his own efforts rather than by God's grace. Sabbath-breakers were punished with death for this very reason.

Unfortunately, Israel's history shows us that the Sabbath eventually became neither a reminder of God's eternal Sabbath rest nor of Israel's redemption from Egypt. By the time of the prophet Nehemiah, the Sabbath had become a day like any other weekday—Israel habitually broke God's rule of love. The Israelites trod their winepresses and brought their grain, wine, grapes, figs, and produce to sell in the market on the day of rest. Aliens in their midst also conducted their business on the Sabbath (Neh. 13:15–18). The Sabbath no longer was a day of rest and worship and celebration of redemption from Egypt but had become a day like any other. Still, God continued to call His people back to honor the Sabbath day:

> If thou turn away thy foot from the sabbath, from doing thy pleasure on my holy day; and call the sabbath a delight, the holy of the LORD, honourable; and shalt honour him, not doing thine own ways, nor finding thine own pleasure, nor speaking thine own words: then shalt thou delight thyself in the LORD; and I will cause thee to ride upon the high places of the earth, and feed thee with the heritage of Jacob thy father: for the mouth of the LORD hath spoken it (Isa. 58:13–14).

Let us now look at how the fourth commandment was fulfilled in the New Testament through the person and work of Christ.

In the Light of Christ

The fourth commandment reflects God as well as Christ in His person, work, and perfect righteousness. Paul makes this point clear: "Let no man therefore judge you in meat, or in drink, or in respect of an holyday, or of the new moon, or of the sabbath days: which are a shadow of things to come; but the body is of Christ" (Col. 2:16–17).

Christ fulfilled the fourth commandment, first, by accomplishing the work that God sent Him to do: "I have glorified thee on the earth: I have finished the work which thou gavest me to do" (John 17:4). Christ cried out on the cross, "It is finished" (John 19:30), indicating that He had accomplished the work His heavenly Father gave Him. Subsequently, Christ ascended to heaven, where He now sits at the right hand of His Father to rule (Heb. 10:12–13). Unlike Adam, Christ entered the rest of God after completing the work that the Father sent Him to do. Prior to Christ, no high priest had entered the holy of holies, then sat down. Each high priest entered the holy of holies, performed his priestly work, then exited the place in peril for his life. Christ, however, sat down after doing His work and rested. The link between Christ and Sabbath rest is especially evident in Luke's gospel, though we must briefly return to the Old Testament to examine other elements of Israel's Sabbath rest to fully realize the link between Christ and Sabbath rest.

Israel celebrated Sabbath rest once a week, but she also had an expanded Sabbath rest once every seven years, and once every fifty years during the year of Jubilee (Lev. 25:1–7; 25:8–19). So God commanded a Sabbath rest once a week, once every seven years, and once every fifty years. In light of this sabbatical pattern, Christ's work is especially significant for the Sabbath. Think, for example, about how Christ stood in the synagogue and read from the scroll of Isaiah:

The Spirit of the Lord is upon me, because he hath anointed me to preach the gospel to the poor; he hath sent me to heal the broken-hearted, to preach deliverance to the captives, and recovering of sight to the blind, to set at liberty them that are bruised, to preach the acceptable year of the Lord. And he closed the book, and he gave it again to the minister, and sat down. And the eyes of all them that were in the synagogue were fastened on him. And he began to say unto them, This day is this scripture fulfilled in your ears (Luke 4:18–21; cf. Isa. 61:1–2).

Christ quoted Isaiah 61:1 in proclaiming the year of Jubilee, then said this extended Sabbath was being fulfilled in Himself. In love, Christ was about to complete the work that the Father had given Him and by this would inaugurate the year of Jubilee. In His life, death, and resurrection, Christ would usher believers into the Jubilee of eternal rest. Thus we no longer worship on Saturday, the last day of the week, but on Resurrection Sunday, the first day of the week, when Jesus rose from the dead.

The Connection to the Church
Israel worked six days, then rested on the last day of the week, because she looked forward to the completion of her workweek. We, on the other

hand, rest first, then work in gratitude for the completed work of Christ. Each Lord's Day, or Sunday, we rest from our labors and celebrate our redemption from the bondage of Satan, sin, and death. Indeed, Sabbath rest is the heartbeat of Christ's offer: "Come unto me, all ye that labour and are heavy laden, and I will give you rest" (Matt. 11:28). We enter eternal rest the same way Israel was supposed to enter Sabbath rest—by faith, not by works.

Israel was to cease from work as a visible recognition that she would enter the eternal Sabbath rest of God by His grace and not by works. So, too, we must cease from our weekday labors to tell our fellow brothers and sisters in Christ and the world around us that we enter the eternal rest of God, not by our works, but by the work of Jesus Christ. In this, we see that the death penalty for disobedience to the fourth commandment is still in effect, for the person who tries to enter God's rest by his own works rather than by faith in the work of Christ, will merit the wages of death, even eternal death. So obedience to the fourth commandment is far more than stopping our daily labors. We see that through Sabbath rest we celebrate the completion of Christ's work in His life, death, and resurrection. We see that the Lord's Day is a celebration of our liberation from bondage to Satan, sin, and death. We see that God does not want to rob us of our joy on the Sabbath but rather wants us to rejoice in our God-given, Christ-wrought, Spirit-applied freedom from slavery to Satan, sin, and death.

With this understanding of the fourth commandment, we may then enter a universe of joy each Lord's Day. Rather than filling ourselves with our own pleasures on Sunday, as the Israelites did in Nehemiah's day, or endlessly laboring without ever knowing any rest, we choose to die to ourselves so we may receive a taste of heaven every Sunday. We do not absent ourselves from corporate worship. We do not starve ourselves of God's Word and fill ourselves with the food of the world. Rather, we come to the temple of God to join the body of Christ and feed upon the manna from heaven, Jesus Christ. If we commemorate holidays, anniversaries, and birthdays with special events and celebrations, should we not likewise celebrate the life, death, and resurrection of Christ on His special day?

What is the best way to observe the Lord's Day? A simple way to answer this is to ask, Does my activity promote or hinder my celebration of the life, death, and resurrection of Christ? Corporate worship, reading the Scriptures, prayer, singing psalms and hymns, meditating upon Christ, fellowshipping with the body of Christ, visiting the sick, and attending the needs of others help us celebrate Christ's work. Watching ballgames, shopping, doing homework, and working around the house do not promote our celebration of Christ's work because these are activities that we do every weekday. They do not help us meditate upon the completed work of Christ.

We should observe the Lord's Day not out of duty or obligation but with joy, celebration, and love for our triune God. So many people consider Sabbath observance as an obligation to be performed, yet they look forward to birthdays, anniversaries, holidays, and other special days. If we can rejoice in such earthly celebrations, shouldn't we rejoice even more on the days that celebrate the work of Christ and our redemption? We should let the words of the prophet Isaiah echo in our minds: "If thou turn away thy foot from the sabbath, from doing thy pleasure on my holy day; and call the sabbath a delight, the holy of the LORD.... I will cause thee to ride upon the high places of the earth" (Isa. 58:13–14).

Conclusion

The fourth commandment reminds us to celebrate the completed work of Christ. Like Israel, we should celebrate the Lord's Day in anticipation of finally and completely entering the eternal day of rest that God Himself entered in Genesis 2:2. The commandment should also remind us that we enter that rest, not by our works, for the wages of sin is death, but by grace through faith in Christ and His work. Let us therefore welcome the fourth commandment as a reminder to mourn our failures to fulfill its demands and to flee to the completed work of Christ. Let us rejoice in the knowledge that Christ has completed the work of the Father on our behalf. Let us also consider the fourth commandment as a guide for holy living, remembering that each Lord's Day offers us a taste of heaven itself. Let us rejoice every Lord's Day until we finally and completely enter the eternal seventh day of God's rest.

STUDY QUESTIONS

1. What are some of the reasons that Christians give for saying that the fourth commandment is no longer binding upon the church?

2. What is the sabbatical pattern that God employed in the Old Testament to mark the passing of days and years?

3. In what way is the eternal rest of God connected with the fourth commandment?

4. In what ways should we observe the Lord's Day?

The Fifth Commandment

In many ways culture is a product of its history; it is defining moments that shape a people. This principle is certainly true of American culture, which was born out of revolution against the policies and rule of England's King George. It appears that this culture-shaping event continues today, for one of American's defining characteristics is its rugged individualism. Autonomous individuals often recoil at the thought of submitting to authority. Yet such individualism, or self-rule, is at odds with a prominent teaching of Scripture to submit to the authority of God and the authorities whom He appoints.

Submitting to authority is the primary focus of the fifth commandment. By keeping in mind the historical, covenantal, and redemptive contexts of this commandment, we will see how it teaches far more than the obedience of children to their parents. We should consider another issue, however, before examining the fifth commandment.

Historically many people have understood that the Ten Commandments are divided into the first and second tables of the Law. The Westminster Confession of Faith, for example, states, "The first four commandments contain our duty towards God; and the other six, our duty to man" (19.2). This division is fostered of course by Christ's explanation of the two greatest commandments: loving God with all of our heart, soul, and mind, and loving our neighbor as ourselves (Matt. 22:37–39). We should acknowledge the general truth of this division of the Law, but at the same time not allow too radical a separation by saying the first four commandments deal exclusively with God and the latter six with man. That simply is not true.

We see, for example, that the fourth commandment instructs Israel to give sons, daughters, slaves, and animals rest on the Sabbath. The fourth commandment thus includes instructions that relate to our duty to God as well as to Christ's second greatest commandment: "Thou shalt love thy neighbour as thyself" (Matt. 22:39). The latter six commandments also include duties to God, not just man. Think, for example, of David's adultery with Bathsheba and murder of Uriah the Hittite; both violated the sixth and seventh commandments. Yet, David also recognized that he had sinned against God in saying, "Against thee, thee only, have I sinned, and done this evil in thy sight" (Ps. 51:4a). We must recognize the interconnected nature of the first and second tables of the Law, for if we do not, we will run the risk of thinking that the last six commandments only deal with our responsibilities to man. If we divorce our duties to man from our duties to God, we will quickly find ourselves in the realm of Godless and Christless ethics, or a set of rules that we believe we can fulfill. We must recognize the vertical element in each of the Ten Commandments, namely our duty to God, which finds completion in the work of Christ. And we must recognize the horizontal element in each commandment, which is our duty to other people. There is a twin focus to God's rule of love: not only a love for God but also a love for our neighbor (Deut. 6:5–6; Lev. 19:18; Matt. 22:37–39). Hopefully, we will see both the vertical and horizontal elements of each commandment. Let us therefore examine the significance of the fifth commandment in how it points to Christ and how it affects us.

In Its Original Setting

The fifth commandment states: "Honour thy father and thy mother: that thy days may be long upon the land which the LORD thy God giveth thee" (Ex. 20:12). The commandment begins with the instruction to honor one's father and mother. To honor one's parents means far more than merely obeying them; it also means giving them precedence, respect, and love. We see something of the great scope of the fifth commandment in Leviticus 19:3, which says, "Ye shall fear every man his mother, and his father, and keep my sabbaths: I am the LORD your God." But what does it mean to fear one's parents?

Throughout Scripture, fear does not always mean being scared. Sometimes it means having a healthy respect or reverence for God or one's parents. Regarding the fear of the Lord, Proverbs 1:7 states: "The fear of the LORD is the beginning of knowledge: but fools despise wisdom and instruction." Likewise, Proverbs 9:10 says, "The fear of the LORD is the beginning of wisdom: and the knowledge of the holy is understanding." Proverbs 3:9 says, "Honour the LORD with thy substance, and with the firstfruits of all thine increase." The very same terms of fear and honor, found in the fifth commandment, are also directed to God.

God considered Israel His firstborn son, which implies that God was Israel's Father (Ex. 4:22). The father-son connection between God and Israel is explicit in other places of Scripture: "A son honoureth his father, and a servant his master: if then I be a father, where is mine honour? and if I be a master, where is my fear? saith the LORD of hosts unto you, O priests, that despise my name'" (Mal. 1:6). Here the terms of honor and fear are applied to God, which is connected to His fatherhood of

Israel. This passage suggests that individual Israelites were to model the relationship between God and Israel of father and child. Just as Israel was to submit to its heavenly Father, so Israelite children were to submit to their parents.

Indeed, parents are God's representatives, standing in God's stead and representing His authority on earth. For this reason, the fifth commandment includes the promise for obedience: "That thy days may be long upon the land which the LORD thy God giveth thee." If Israel was obedient, if she loved her God, the Lord would bless her and allow her to remain in the Promised Land. If she disobeyed, however, and broke God's rule of love, God would eject her from the land. Obedience was required of adults but also of the sons and daughters of Israel. As Israel herself submitted to her Father, so her children should submit to their parents, God's representatives on earth. By now we should sense some elements in this commandment that point us to the person and work of Christ.

The Connection to Christ and the Church

We must not divorce the first and second tables of the Law in their duties to God and man, because they are inextricably linked. Hopefully we will also remember that the Law is not only a reflection of God's character and attributes but also a reflection of Christ's obedience and perfect righteousness. The connection between the first and second tables

of the Law becomes clear when we consider that
Adam was God's son, but he disobeyed his heavenly Father, which resulted in his exile from the
garden of Eden. Likewise, Israel was God's child
but was disobedient to her heavenly Father, which
resulted in her exile from the Promised Land. Now
let us consider how Christ, the only begotten Son
of God, was obedient to the will of His heavenly
Father. He fulfilled God's rule of love through His
obedient submission to the Father.

Christ's obedience is evident in His forty-day
wilderness experience, which is evocative of Israel's forty-year wandering in the wilderness prior
to entering the Land of Canaan. But we should
also note Christ's obedience in the garden of Gethsemane, where He wrestled with His Father's
will prior to His crucifixion (Matt. 26:39). Christ
consistently sought to honor His Father (John
8:48–49). Indeed, throughout His life on earth,
Christ honored His heavenly Father. Such obedience caused Paul to write: "Being found in fashion
as a man, he humbled himself, and became obedient unto death, even the death of the cross" (Phil.
2:8). Christ's obedience means that we must obey
the fifth commandment beyond the usual reasons
cited such as: "Because God has commanded,"
or "Because God has established parents as His
authorities in the life of children."

We should obey the fifth commandment because parents are God's established authorities over their children. We should also obey the fifth commandment because Christ has redeemed us from the bondage of sin and death, and we are now being renewed in the image of Christ (Rom. 8:29). We are enabled to love God because He has first loved us (1 John 4:19). In love we must submit to the authority of our heavenly Father just as Christ submitted to His Father. Such submission is central in Paul's instructions to the Philippians (2:5–8), where he urges the Philippians to have the mind of Christ, who obeyed His Father. For this reason Paul repeats the fifth commandment in his epistle to the Ephesians, saying, "Children, obey your parents in the Lord: for this is right. Honour thy father and mother; (which is the first commandment with promise;) that it may be well with thee, and thou mayest live long on the earth" (Eph. 6:1–3).

Paul also tells children to obey their parents, "in the Lord," which emphasizes that parents represent God's authority. Paul gives the same instruction to wives, saying, "Wives, submit yourselves unto your own husbands, as unto the Lord" (Eph. 5:22). He gives slaves similar instruction: "Servants, be obedient to them that are your masters according to the flesh, with fear and trembling, in singleness of your heart, as unto Christ" (Eph. 6:5). Hence, while the fifth commandment speaks specifically about honoring parents, it may be more broadly applied to any God-instituted authority: husbands, parents, elders in the church, employers, and representatives of civil government. We must understand, however, why we should submit to authority. Paul says we must submit "one to another in the fear of God" (Eph. 5:21), and we must "be filled with the Spirit" (Eph. 5:18). Thus those who are filled with the Holy Spirit and reverence God are the ones who obey His Law, submitting to God's authority in whatever form they find it.

A Christ-centered approach to the fifth commandment teaches us that we, the people of God, who are being remade in the image of Christ, must honor our fathers and mothers and any other God-instituted authority because we are to reflect the perfect righteousness and love of Christ. This commandment is not restricted to elders of the church, parents, or children. Rather, all of God's people, from the least to the greatest, must reflect the righteousness of Christ. Children must obey their parents because they are the God-ordained authorities who feed, clothe, care for, and love them, but also because children have been born within the covenant and have been set apart by God to reflect the glory of Jesus Christ. Children therefore will shine forth the glory of Christ when they obey their parents. Wives will shine forth the glory of Christ when they submit to their husbands. Husbands will shine forth the glory of Christ when they submit to the authority of Christ. Husbands, wives, and children will exhibit the glory of Christ when they submit to the elders of the church. And elders of the church will shine forth the glory of Christ when they submit to the authority of Christ.

Must we always obey our parents, husband, church elders, or God-instituted authority? Because of the presence of sin in the world, there is a significant difference between the submission and honor of Christ to His Father and our submission and honor to earthly authority. Christ did not fear that His Father's will was sinful because God is perfectly holy, whereas earthly authorities such as parents, husbands, elders, and governments sin. Sometimes an authority imposes laws upon us that are contrary to the Word of God. We see an example of this in Daniel when Nebuchadnezzar declared an edict for everyone to worship an idol. Daniel rightfully opposed this edict (Daniel 3). Similarly, a child may reach a point sometime in life when he puts Christ before parents for the greater obedience of God (Luke 14:26). Typically when an earthly authority usurps the supreme authority of Christ, we must follow Jesus rather than man.

Then, too, in the natural order of things, a son or daughter may leave the authority of parents to become an authority in his or her own home. The son or daughter is always under the authority of the church, however, and a daughter might move under the authority of a husband. At that point, the relationship between child and parent becomes one of respect, care, and love, not of direct obedience. One more thing: we may not rebel against authority if we think it is heavy-handed or unjust. We may disobey authority only if it imposes sinful demands upon us. Christ Himself submitted to harsh and cruel authority in His suffering and death (1 Pet. 3:1–2). It is one thing for an authority to be harsh—to impose heavy taxes, strict rules in the home, or require the performance of many household duties and chores. In these circumstances, humble submission, respect, and honor are required, just as Christ Himself suffered under unjust authority. It is entirely another matter for an authority to refuse to let a subordinate, a constituent, employee, wife, or child read the Word or go to church. In these circumstances, humble but resolute disobedience to earthly authority is required because it is ultimately obedience to Christ our husband, and God our heavenly Father.

Conclusion

How many of us violate the fifth commandment in failing to obey and honor representatives of civil government? Do we obey and honor church authorities? Wives, do you obey and honor your husbands? Children, do you obey and honor your parents? Employees, do you obey and honor your employers? In the end, we must admit that we repeatedly fail to obey the fifth commandment. The Law condemns our disobedience, yet we also know that it drives us to Christ, who was truly obedient in giving honor to His heavenly Father. May we look to Christ's obedience, knowing it is the perfect righteousness that we are to reflect through the power of the Holy Spirit as those who bear the image of Christ, and in whom the Spirit is applying the rule of love.

STUDY QUESTIONS

1. How is the Law divided into two tables?

2. Are the first and second tables of the Law mutually exclusive?

3. In what way does Israel's father-son relationship with God anticipate Christ's relationship with God?

4. To whom does the scope of the fifth commandment extend?

5. When is disobedience to superiors permitted?

The Sixth Commandment

We may have become desensitized to the horrific nature of murder because we so often see it reported in the news, hear of soldiers killed in combat, or see death glibly portrayed in other forms of media. Yet many people think they have never come close to committing murder because they have not raised a hand in anger against another. Having never done serious physical harm to anyone, they believe they are free from the guilt of murder. By reflecting upon the sixth commandment within its historical, covenantal, and redemptive contexts as well as taking into account the interconnected nature of the two tables of the Law, we will see how this commandment goes far beyond mere outward actions to plumb the depths of our hearts.

In Its Original Setting

The sixth commandment states, "Thou shalt not kill" (Ex. 20:13). The commandment seems simple enough but what does it mean? It does not mean that taking life in any situation is wrong. The Hebrew term, which the King James Version of the Bible translates as "kill," is not the same term used in contexts of war or in the just punishment of a crime. In our day, the term refers to premeditated murder, first and second degree murder, or voluntary manslaughter, not taking life in war or executing a criminal for a capital offense. Nevertheless, the Hebrew term here does include the unintentional killing of someone in what we would call involuntary manslaughter. But the term is never used in connection with the death of animals; it only deals with the death of people.

Every society since the beginning of history has viewed murder as evil. This universal consent suggests why we must not look at the second table of the Law exclusively in terms of our duty to mankind. If the commandment is merely a prohibition against murder, then it is not unique, since most if not all cultures prohibit murder. If we consider the vertical, or God-ward, dimension of this law, however, we soon see how this commandment is different from all other cultural norms. We see the God-ward dimension of the command not to kill early in the Scriptures: "Whoso sheddeth man's blood, by man shall his blood be shed: for in the image of God made he man" (Gen. 9:6). Killing is far more than a sin against our fellow man; it attacks and dishonors the very image of God. Murder is an attack on God Himself.

We can also appreciate the significance of this commandment within the context of Israel's exodus from Egypt. Through the sixth commandment God was telling His people that murder was incompatible with their redemption from slavery. Recall, it was Pharaoh who ordered the murder of all Israelite male infants. By contrast, Old Testament Israel was commanded to respect and revere the lives of people who were inside or outside the covenant. Their reverence for life was rooted not only in respect for their neighbor but ultimately in respect for God and His redemptive grace, which freed them from the oppression of murder; and for God's image, because man is made in the image of God.

We must thus recognize both the horizontal and vertical elements of the sixth commandment. At the same time, we must not think that obedience to this commandment consists simply of refraining from taking the life of another. That was a common belief in the time of Christ, and it persists today. We must consider the commandment in its original context in the Decalogue but also in terms of what Christ said about this commandment. Christ said, "Whosoever is angry with his brother without a cause shall be in danger of the judgment: and whosoever shall say to his brother, Raca, shall be in danger of the council: but whosoever shall say, Thou fool, shall be in danger of hell fire" (Matt. 5:22). Some people think that Christ elevated the requirements of the sixth commandment here. We do not have space here to refute that. Suffice it to say that Christ does not expand the requirements of the commandment; rather, He authoritatively interprets it. And Christ's interpretation was what God intended when He gave the commandment to Moses on Mount Sinai.

Notice that Christ says a person is guilty of violating the sixth commandment if he is simply angry with another believer. Indeed, all we must do is insult a brother or sister in Christ and we are guilty of violating the sixth commandment. How can this be? Once again, if we look merely at the horizontal application of this commandment, we might find all sorts of reasons to justify our anger or insults toward another believer. However, James says about our tongue: "Therewith bless we God, even the Father; and therewith curse we men, which are made after the similitude of God" (James 3:9). Once again we see that the reason for not expressing anger or insults to a fellow believer is rooted in the image of God. To be angry or to insult another believer is to attack God Himself. Furthermore, anger and hate are the roots of murder. Indeed, the Law judges not only our actions but also our motives, which, in this case, are the hatred and anger that lead to murder—the very antithesis of love. The apostle John explains the implications of disobeying the sixth commandment when he says: "Whosoever hateth his brother is a murderer: and ye know that no murderer hath eternal life abiding in him" (1 John 3:15).

The Connection to Christ and the Church

The Law of God not only reflects His being and attributes but also the perfect righteousness of Jesus Christ. We must look not only at Christ's authoritative interpretation of this commandment but also at His fulfillment of it. Christ came not to abolish the Law or the prophets but to fulfill them (Matt. 5:17). Christ certainly never committed an act of murder. Not only was Christ innocent of murder but He was Himself a murder victim. In his Pentecost sermon, Peter said wicked hands had crucified and slain Jesus (Acts 2:23). Yet Christ was innocent of any sin (Heb. 4:15; cf. James 2:10). Indeed, Christ came to fulfill the Law in every way. Christ's obedience was perfect. He did not commit murder but He also did not express hatred or unrighteous anger against anyone. Rather, He loved a people who hated Him (Rom. 5:1–8). Christ was angry, but it was a righteous and holy anger (cf. Eph. 4:26).

What is amazing is that in spite of His perfect fulfillment of the Law, Christ willingly suffered the curse and penalty of the Law on our behalf—we who have broken God's rule of love (Deut. 21:22–23; cf. Gal. 3:13). Though Christ never violated the sixth commandment, He willingly suffered on the cross as one who was guilty. He suffered and died on our behalf so that we, who are guilty of breaking the sixth commandment, would not have to suffer the wrath of God for our murderous conduct. Christ's death on the cross reveals why murder and hate are incompatible with our redemption. God's redemption of Israel from the murderous tyranny of a despot was one reason why Israel was forbidden to murder. The other reason was that in committing murder or hating someone, they would attack the image of the very God who had redeemed them from bondage.

In a far greater way, Christ has redeemed us from the bondage of sin and death. He has redeemed us from the tyranny of the murderous despotic ruler, Satan, who "was a murderer from the beginning" (John 8:44). In addition, we have been redeemed to reflect the image of Christ (Col. 3:9–10). Christ perfectly obeyed the Law and neither murdered nor hated anyone. He respected the image of our heavenly Father, even when those who bore that image were guilty of the vilest hatred towards Christ (Luke 23:34). Christ has redeemed us from the bondage of sin and death, not so we can continue to walk in the former ways of sin but so we may walk in newness of

life. Accordingly, Christ tells us that we are to love
our enemies, not hate them (Matt. 5:43–38).

We are also commanded to love those who
express hate toward us. Love for our brothers and
sisters in Christ and for our enemies marks us as
children of Christ (1 John 2:9–11). God loved us
in Christ, even when we were His enemies (Rom.
5:6–8). So the sixth commandment is not simply a prohibition against murder. In the light of
Christ, the commandment is a powerful incentive
to unconditionally love others—the divine application of the rule of love.

We have been redeemed and renewed in the
image of Christ so that we may shine forth the
glory of Christ by manifesting the love of Christ
to all people, even those who are our enemies. We
do that because God has done this for us in Christ,
showing His love to His bitter enemies who seethed
with hatred and murder for their Creator. Oh that
we as the people of God would reflect the perfect
righteousness of Christ in this prohibition against
murder! We live at a time when sarcasm is the
norm and insults are common. Yet that kind of
behavior is incompatible with the image of Christ
that we bear. Even if we do not insult someone to
his face, our heavenly Father still feels the assault
upon His image. Do we harbor bitterness and
hatred for our brother or sister? Are we dishonest
about our feelings and cloak our hatred under the
guise of merely disliking a person? Those around

us may not be aware of our feelings, but our omniscient heavenly Father is well aware of our assault upon His image.

Do we in the church respect all human life, which means respecting the image of God? Or do we remain silent on matters such as abortion, euthanasia, or suicide? The church's greatest sin against the sixth commandment has not been in the public square but rather within the church itself. Statistics indicate there is little difference in the number of abortions among unbelievers and that among professing Christians. Those statistics will never change unless people in the church seriously believe that they bear the image of Christ and that murder is incompatible with that image. The church is a covenant community that must respect every form of life, whether an unborn child, the elderly, or the mentally, emotionally, or psychologically troubled. In our respect for life, we must show that we respect the image of God by shining forth the love of Christ for one another.

Conclusion

A true understanding of the sixth commandment makes us aware of how frequently we violate this command. Let us hear the loud thunder of the Law of God as it accuses and condemns us. Then let us flee to Christ, who has stilled the Law's thunder by fulfilling its requirements and suffering its penalty on our behalf. Remember that we have been redeemed and are being remade in the image of Christ. We must therefore walk in newness of life. We must love others as Christ has loved us.

STUDY QUESTIONS

1. When the commandment says, "Thou shalt not kill," what type of sin does it specifically have in view?

2. How is the murder of another human being an attack upon God?

3. How did Christ fulfill the sixth commandment?

4. In what way is hate a violation of the sixth commandment?

The Seventh Commandment

Adultery is a term that has virtually disappeared from our culture. Many people reason, "If God wants me to be happy, and my spouse makes me sad, then I should find happiness elsewhere, even if it means breaking my vows to be faithful in marriage." With this twisted reasoning, thousands, if not millions, justify their conduct. Adultery is no longer discussed as sin or wickedness but merely as "inappropriate behavior." How wrong that is! Inappropriate behavior is wearing blue jeans to a black tie dinner; adultery is sin! But as with other commandments, many people think they are free from violating the seventh commandment if they simply do not physically engage in sexual conduct outside of marriage. If we recognize the God-ward dimension of the commandment as well as its historical, covenantal, and redemptive contexts, we soon realize that the seventh commandment requires far more of us.

In Its Original Setting

The seventh commandment states, "Thou shalt not commit adultery" (Ex. 20:14). In its original setting, this commandment was a prohibition against violating the sanctity of the marriage covenant. The primary way of violating the marriage covenant was being sexually unfaithful to a spouse, that is, having sexual intercourse with the spouse of another. The prohibition against adultery appears in other places in Scripture, such as: "Thou shalt not lie carnally with thy neighbour's wife, to defile thyself with her" (Lev. 18:20; cf. Hos. 4:13). The commandment applied to engagement as well as marriage, for whether married or engaged, one who violated this commandment was subject to the death penalty (Deut. 22:22–24). Yet the intent of this commandment goes beyond the preservation of the sanctity of engagement or marriage.

According to Christ's interpretation of the Law, this commandment involves both actions and motives. Jesus said, "Ye have heard that it was said by them of old time, Thou shalt not commit adultery: but I say unto you, That whosoever looketh on a woman to lust after her hath committed adultery with her already in his heart" (Matt. 5:27–28). Thus the mere contemplation of sexual immorality violates the seventh commandment.

In addition, a person can also commit adultery
by obtaining an unbiblical divorce, for Jesus said,
"It hath been said, Whosoever shall put away his
wife, let him give her a writing of divorcement: but
I say unto you, That whosoever shall put away
his wife, saving for the cause of fornication, caus-
eth her to commit adultery: and whosoever shall
marry her that is divorced committeth adultery"
(Matt. 5:31–32). Divorcing for anything less than
biblical grounds means that in the eyes of God the
marriage is still valid. Thus by engaging in sexual
intercourse with anyone else each spouse commits
adultery. Note here that the requirements of God's
Law are often more demanding than the legal
requirements of a state. While one may legally
obtain a certificate of divorce on the grounds of
irreconcilable differences, the Bible does not recognize these grounds as legitimate for divorce. So,
a divorce may be lawful in the eyes of the state,
but before the throne of God, the legality of the
divorce is entirely a different matter.

What makes this commandment unique from
the practices of other cultures in the days of
Moses? Most if not all cultures during the time
of the Decalogue had prohibitions against adultery. The answer once again is the vertical nature
of the commandment. Under God's Law, we cannot divorce our obligations to people from our
covenant relationship with God. What sets this
commandment apart from laws of other cultures is

that others view adultery only as a crime between people whereas in Israel the crime is also against God. It is like the fifth commandment, which not only deals with the obedience of children to their parents but also with the obedience of Israel to her Father God (Ex. 4:22).

The image of God as husband and Israel as unfaithful wife is prominent in the book of Hosea. It is repeated in Isaiah 57:1–13, Ezekiel 23:36–49, and Jeremiah 3:6–9. Indeed throughout the Old Testament, Israel's idolatry is likened to men gathering at a whorehouse (Jer. 5:7). The seventh commandment deals with the sanctity of marriage here on earth as well as Israel's marriage to God. Just as Old Testament Israelites were to be faithful to one another in both thought and deed within marriage, they were to be faithful to their covenant Lord.

The Connection to Christ and the Church

Christ the faithful and sacrificial husband

When we look at the Law, we must see the character and attributes of God as well as the perfect righteousness of Jesus Christ. So we must consider not only Christ's authoritative teaching and interpretation but also His person and work. In this respect Jesus Christ is the bridegroom and we, the church, are His bride. Paul makes clear this connection between Christ and the church in Ephesians 5 when he writes: "Husbands, love your wives, even as Christ also loved the church, and gave himself for it; that he might sanctify and cleanse it with the washing of water by the word, that he might present it to himself a glorious church, not having spot, or wrinkle, or any such thing; but that it should be holy and without blemish" (Eph. 5:25–27). Notice that husbands are to love their wives as Christ loves the church.

Christ is faithful in every way to His bride, the church; He has fulfilled the rule of love. He cleanses her from all of sin so that in the eyes of God she is holy and without blemish. The significance of marriage, then, must be seen in light of Christ's marriage to His bride, the church. As Paul explains,

> So ought men to love their wives as their own bodies. He that loveth his wife loveth himself. For no man ever yet hated his own flesh; but nourisheth and cherisheth it, even as the Lord the church: For we are members of his body, of his flesh, and of his bones. For this cause shall a man leave his father and mother, and shall be joined unto his wife, and they two shall be one flesh. This is a great mystery: but I speak concerning Christ and the church (Eph. 5:28–32).

In this passage Paul refers back to Genesis 2:24, saying that God's creation of the first husband and wife was a portrait of the relationship between His Son, Jesus Christ, and His bride, the church. Paul calls this relationship of marriage a mystery because its purpose was once hidden but now has been revealed with the advent of Christ (cf. Rom. 16:25–26a). Christ's relationship with the church sheds important light upon the seventh commandment. I think we are prone to look at the commandments of God as if He were stingy and only had our misery in mind when He revealed His Law at Sinai. We should rather view the commandment as a reflection of Christ's faithfulness and love to and for us, the church, as His bride. The connection between Christ and the seventh commandment thus has many implications for the way we should live as people being remade in the image of Christ—as a people in whom the rule of love is being applied by Christ through the Spirit.

Our faithfulness to Christ

We must first realize that we are married to Christ (Rom. 7:1–4) and thus must be faithful to Him. We must not, like Old Testament Israel, deal faithlessly with God our husband and break the bond of love. We must not commit spiritual adultery by worshiping other gods. As Paul says, we have been joined to Christ so that we may bear fruit for God.

Our marriages

The seventh commandment says our marriages should reflect the righteousness of Christ. If marriage was created to emulate Christ and the church, then we should ask how our marriages reflect Christ and the church. The answer is that we must shine forth as Christ and the church in our marriages. Adultery and divorce are at odds with the Christian's identity in Christ. God hates both adultery and divorce. He does not give the seventh commandment to ruin our lives or make us unhappy. Rather, He wants us to reflect the faithfulness of God and Christ. Christ does not abandon His bride, the church, or commit adultery, and He will never divorce her. When we commit adultery or divorce a spouse for unbiblical reasons, we tell the world that Christ also commits adultery and divorces His wife, the church.

What kind of message do our marriages send to the world? Far from merely abstaining from adultery, we must nourish our marriages with sacrificial love. Indeed, we should think of the faithfulness of Christ when we read the seventh commandment and how we are called to manifest the love of Christ in our marriages. When we read the seventh commandment, we should not simply read, "Thou shalt not commit adultery," but also, "You should love your spouse with the sacrificial love of Christ."

Our sexual conduct

We must not think that the seventh commandment only applies to married people. Remember, Christ says this commandment applies to actions as well as motives of the heart. So, whether married or single, all believers are married to Christ. We must thus be faithful to Christ and be obedient to what He commands, regardless of our marital status. Indeed, since we are being renewed in Christ's image, we are to reflect the righteousness of Christ. Whether we are single or married, our sexual conduct should reflect the righteousness of Christ.

Do we engage in adulterous conduct in our thoughts? Adulterous conduct can be fueled by what we see. Do we look with lust at people we see in film, on the pages of a magazine, on the computer screen, or even in the supermarket? Several years ago a large conservative denomination held its annual meetings at a convention center. The local newspaper noted that in-room subscription to pornographic movies by conventioneers during that time was no different from that of people at any other convention.

Does our sexual conduct encourage others to stumble? What about what we wear—does it entice others to lust after our bodies? While the issue of modesty is certainly applicable to both men and women, I think it applies more specifically to women today. As 1 Peter 3:3–4 says: "Whose adorning let it not be that outward adorning of plaiting the hair, and of wearing of gold, or of putting on of apparel; but let it be the hidden man of the heart, in that which is not corruptible, even the ornament of a meek and quiet spirit, which is in the sight of God of great price" (1 Pet. 3:3–4). Women, does your clothing entice men to stumble? In all matters that pertain to our sexual conduct, we must reflect the righteousness of Christ.

Conclusion

The seventh commandment convicts us that we are guilty of idolatry and abandoning Christ, our faithful husband. It tells us we are guilty of adulterous thoughts, sexual misconduct, and unbiblical divorce. It tells us we fail to love Christ and our spouses as we should. Beloved, when we sense the Law's condemnation, let us flee to Christ, the faithful one who never looked at a woman with lust, who was never guilty of sexual misconduct, and who has been faithful to His bride, the church, loving her and laying down His life for her. As Paul says, Christ has cleansed, washed, and sanctified us. He has borne the condemnation of the Law on our behalf and freed us from its curse. As Paul tells us, we have been freed from the Law and are married to one another so that we can bear fruit unto God. Let us therefore strive to shine forth the image of Christ, which renews us day by day in our marriage to Christ, our marriage to our spouses, and in our sexual conduct.

STUDY QUESTIONS

1. Does the seventh commandment only address our sexual conduct?

2. Must a person physically violate the marriage covenant to transgress the seventh commandment?

3. In what way is Christ a faithful husband?

4. In what way does the seventh commandment apply to those who are not married?

5. Does the commandment merely tell us to abstain from adultery? How should we treat our spouses?

The Eighth Commandment

Most everyone agrees that theft is wrong. True, thieves may have few qualms with stealing the possession of others. However, even thieves may feel offended when other thieves steal from them. "Steal from someone else but never from me!" they say. But the eighth commandment goes far beyond the physical act of stealing. If we coordinate the second table of the Law with our duty to God as well as man, then we will see that this commandment reaches into our hearts and says much about how we regard God's providential care. If we explore this commandment in terms of its historical, covenantal, and redemptive contexts, we will see how it leads us to Christ and His bride, the church.

In its Original Setting

The eighth commandment says, "Thou shalt not steal" (Ex. 20:15). The commandment seems simple enough; the Israelites should not take what does not belong to them. At the same time, the Old Testament applies this commandment to a wide range of issues. Let us briefly explore some of the issues addressed by the eighth commandment so that we can more fully appreciate its scope within its original context.

Kidnapping

The first issue addressed by this commandment was kidnapping. Stealing another person by taking him or her by force was punishable by death, for Exodus 21:16 said, "And he that stealeth a man, and selleth him, or if he be found in his hand, he shall surely be put to death." So kidnapping a person, then selling him or her into slavery, violated the eighth commandment. Joseph's brothers selling him into slavery readily comes to mind (Genesis 37ff). Although Joseph's brothers did not kill him, they nonetheless violated the eighth commandment, an act which, according to later Israelite legislation, would have been punishable by death (cf. 1 Tim. 1:8–10).

Land

The Israelites would also be guilty of violating the eighth commandment if they took land that did not belong to them. People might steal land by moving property markers, which was the equivalent of moving a fence line today. If you moved a fence a foot into your neighbor's yard, you would then own the land according to the law that said possession was nine-tenths of the law. Job commented on the unlawful practice of moving landmarks as well as stealing the livestock of a neighbor, saying, "Why, seeing times are not hidden from the Almighty, do they that know him not see his days? Some remove the landmarks; they violently take away flocks, and feed thereof" (Job 24:1–2).

Animals

Stealing livestock also violated the eighth commandment, though this crime did not reap the stiff penalty that kidnapping did. Exodus 22:1 said, "If a man shall steal an ox, or a sheep, and kill it, or sell it; he shall restore five oxen for an ox, and four sheep for a sheep."

Wages

Another way to violate the commandment was failing to give employees a fair wage. The prophet Jeremiah condemned those who cheated laborers this way by saying: "Woe unto him that buildeth his house by unrighteousness, and his chambers by wrong; that useth his neighbour's service without wages, and giveth him not for his work"

(Jer. 22:13). In other words, failing to give wages that were rightly due was a form of stealing (cf. James 5:4).

False weights and measures — *Proverbs*

In Old Testament times, merchants in Israel used scales to measure grain, gold, silver, or other commodities. Dishonest merchants would have two sets of weights: an accurate set, which they used when they did not want to be cheated themselves; and a bogus set, which they used to cheat others. Deuteronomy 25:13–15 warned against such dishonest practices, saying:

> Thou shalt not have in thy bag divers weights, a great and a small. Thou shalt not have in thine house divers measures, a great and a small. But thou shalt have a perfect and just weight, a perfect and just measure shalt thou have: that thy days may be lengthened in the land which the LORD thy God giveth thee.

Summary

Kidnapping, stealing livestock, moving land markers, taking the possessions of others, withholding due wages, and using false weights and measures were all violations of the eighth commandment. According to the Westminster Larger Catechism, sins against the eighth commandment included the following:

The sins forbidden in the eighth commandment, besides the neglect of the duties required, are, theft, robbery, man stealing, and receiving any thing that is stolen; fraudulent dealing, false weights and measures, removing land-marks, injustice and unfaithfulness in contracts between man and man, or in matters of trust; oppression, extortion, usury, bribery, vexatious lawsuits, unjust enclosures and depopulations; engrossing commodities to enhance the price; unlawful callings, and all other unjust or sinful ways of taking or withholding from our neighbor what belongs to him, or of enriching ourselves; covetousness; inordinate prizing and affecting worldly goods; distrustful and distracting cares and studies in getting, keeping, and using them; envying at the prosperity of others; as likewise idleness, prodigality, wasteful gaming; and all other ways whereby we do unduly prejudice our own outward estate, and defrauding ourselves of the due use and comfort of that estate which God hath given us (Q. 142).

The scope of the eighth commandment is broad. Nevertheless, we must ask, in what way is this commandment unique? If all societies and cultures recognize the evil of stealing, what sets Israel's law apart? The answer, of course, is the God-ward, or vertical, dimension of the Law.

Vertical dimension

In every other culture, stealing is viewed as an act committed against man. It is thus purely horizontal in nature. For Israel, however, stealing was also a sin against God. When we realize that God has created everything that we see, we must conclude that everything in creation belongs to Him. The psalmist, for example, wrote: "The earth is the LORD's and the fullness thereof" (Ps. 24:1). When Job was struck with calamity and all of his possessions were taken away, he did not complain about losing his property because he recognized that all of it ultimately belonged to the Lord: "Naked came I out of my mother's womb, and naked shall I return thither: the LORD gave, and the LORD hath taken away; blessed be the name of the LORD" (Job 1:21). So, then, taking the possessions of another was akin to taking what belonged to God. Theft was ultimately a crime committed against God, the true owner of all things.

When we consider that God liberated Israel from bondage and slavery in Egypt, we begin to appreciate why kidnapping reaped such a heavy punishment. God did not liberate Israel from bondage only to see her perpetuate this same sin against others. So, even in cases of voluntary slavery, when a person agreed to become a bond-servant because he could not pay his debts, God planned for his release from bondage in the year of Jubilee (Lev. 25:11, 16).

Prince of
Egypt

In the Light of Christ

In the Law we see the perfect righteousness of God and Jesus Christ. We affirm that Christ fulfilled every jot and tittle of the Law, as He Himself testified, saying He came not to destroy the Law and the prophets but to fulfill them (Matt. 5:17). Moreover, the New Testament continually refers to Christ's sinlessness. But in what way did Christ fufill the demands of the eighth commandment? The answer, I believe, is in Philippians 2:5–11, where Paul wrote that Christ "thought it not robbery to be equal with God" (Phil. 2:6). Instead, "He humbled himself, and became obedient unto death, even the death of the cross" (Phil. 2:8). When we think about Christ's obedience to the will of His Father, we must see this in comparison to the disobedience of the first Adam. In the Garden of Eden, Adam took what God had not given him. The first man saw forbidden fruit and took it, thinking that would give him equality with God. He could help himself to whatever he wanted from every other tree in the garden, yet Adam wanted fruit from the only tree that God had denied him.

Christ, though equal with God, did not count His equality with God something to be grasped. He considered that "robbery," as the King James states. Satan tempted Christ in the wilderness to create food, worship Satan, and throw Himself from the top of the temple (Matt. 4:1–11). In all three temptations, Jesus was offered a shortcut to power, possessions, and authority. He could love and obey God the Father and receive from Him the kingdom covenanted to Him, but He could only receive that though suffering and dying on the cross. Or He could bypass the cross by creating bread, bowing to Satan, and immediately receive the kingdoms of the world.

Our heavenly Father told His Son that He was not to eat, so Christ did not reach for what was not rightfully His. In each temptation Christ refrained from taking what did not belong to Him. Moreover, He gave back what rightfully belonged to His Father. Christ fulfilled every aspect of the Law, thereby fulfilling all the requirements of each commandment.

The Connection to the Church

In Philippians 2:5, Paul said, "Let this mind be in you, which was also in Christ Jesus." In other words, the same righteousness that marks Christ is to mark us because we are united to Him through the indwelling power and presence of the Holy Spirit, and we are being renewed into His holy and righteous image. Our desire should not be to take what does not belong to us. To do so is to question the benevolence and providential will of our heavenly Father. We must not take what is not ours, no matter how small: a few pennies, a few minutes from the company, a few miles on the company car, or anything else. Paul addressed

an answer on a test

this type of stealing when he told Titus that slaves were to be submissive to their masters in everything, specifically in not pilfering (Titus 2:9–10).

But this commandment teaches more. Since everything belongs to the Lord, and He is so generous in providing our liberation from slavery to sin and death, we must also be generous with our time and possessions. As the Heidelberg Catechism states: "That I further my neighbor's profit wherever I can or may, deal with him as I would have others deal with me, and labor faithfully that I may be able to relieve the needy" (Q. 111). If we truly value the riches of heaven and God's immeasurable love towards us in Christ, we will not take what does not belong to us and belongs instead to God, but we will recognize how generous He has been with us. By the sanctifying power of the Holy Spirit, our desire will be to share our possessions, time, and money with others. Our desire will be to love our neighbors.

Conclusion

We should not restrict the scope of the eighth commandment to an injunction against thievery. Rather, we must flee to Christ, knowing that we are guilty of violating this commandment in so many ways but that He has fulfilled all righteousness, every jot and tittle, on our behalf. At the same time, we must remember that we are being renewed in the image of Christ daily and that because of our union with Him we are not to steal from others, for to do so is to ultimately steal from God, and this is contrary to our identity as image bearers of Christ. It is contrary to the rule of love. Rather than taking from others, we must be generous with our possessions, freely giving our time, money, and belongings as we reflect the generosity, kindness, and love that our heavenly Father and Savior have given to us. We should not steal but give abundantly of all that we possess, for Christ has so loved us.

STUDY QUESTIONS

1. What are some of the ways that an Israelite could violate the eighth commandment?

2. In what way did Christ fulfill this commandment?

3. How does theft dishonor God's providential care for His people?

4. How is contentment in Christ related to the eighth commandment?

The Ninth Commandment

We live in a world where people fudge numbers on their tax returns, advertisers state half-truths about their products, and governments shade the truth by hiding things from the media. In one sense, our world simply echoes the effects of the serpent's half-truths when he convinced our first parents to disobey God's command and eat the forbidden fruit of the tree of knowledge. The ninth commandment, however, points us in another direction. When we take into account the three contexts (historical, covenantal, and redemptive) of this commandment, we see how it points us to our duties to man and God as well as to the truth incarnate, Jesus Christ. It also shows us how we as the church must reflect the truth of Jesus in both word and deed.

In Its Original Setting

The ninth commandment says, "Thou shalt not bear false witness against thy neighbour" (Ex. 20:16). The original setting of this commandment is giving testimony in a court of law. Exodus 23:1 states what it means to bear false witness against one's neighbor: "Thou shalt not raise a false report: put not thine hand with the wicked to be an unrighteous witness." The Israelites were not to lie in court to favor either the rich or the poor, nor were judges to accept bribes (Ex. 23:6–8). Honesty in court dealings was absolutely necessary to maintain order in Israel as well as in any society. If the courts are corrupt, there can be no justice, and without justice there will be no peace. Total anarchy will ensue. At the same time, we must recognize that the extent of the ninth commandment goes far beyond societal order.

The ninth commandment speaks about the preservation of truth, especially as it pertains to our neighbor. If we lie about our neighbor, we besmirch his character. Thus the ninth commandment tells us to preserve the character of our neighbor. Christ's summation of the law in the second greatest commandment speaks well to this aspect of the ninth commandment: "Thou shalt love thy neighbour as thyself" (Matt. 22:39). We would not want our own character assassinated in a public setting so why would we perpetrate such a sin upon others? We must realize, though, that the ninth commandment extends beyond the court setting to other situations in life.

Recall that many community matters in Israel's day were not resolved in court before a judge but at the gates of the city with the elders. Such was the case with Boaz, who went to the elders of the city to ask permission to take Ruth as his wife (Ruth 4:1–2). In such circumstances honesty was paramount since a person could easily be defrauded or have his character assaulted in such a setting. Because honesty was expected in every situation, the prophet Hosea condemned the Israelites, not just for bearing false witness but also for lying, saying: "There is no truth, nor mercy, nor knowledge of God in the land. By swearing, and lying, and killing, and stealing, and committing adultery, they break out, and blood toucheth blood" (Hos. 4:1–2). Notice that the other sins Hosea mentions are clearly from the Ten Commandments. Thus, while the ninth commandment primarily refers to the court setting, it does not exclude warnings against deceit in general. We also see that Scripture condemns deceit that is offered in jest: "As a mad man who casteth firebrands, arrows, and death, so is the man that deceiveth his neighbour, and saith, Am not I in sport?" (Prov. 26:18–19). So the commandment extends far beyond the court setting in its application.

As we have asked of other commandments from the second table of the Law, we must ask

in what way is the ninth commandment unique?
What makes Israel's prohibition against bearing
false witness and deceit different from the prohibition of surrounding cultures? We must remember
that God called Israel to be His witnesses to the
world, "Ye shall be unto me a kingdom of priests,
and an holy nation" (Ex. 19:6a). If Israel was dishonest, untrustworthy, and deceitful, how could
other nations accept her testimony regarding the
one true God? Moreover, if Israel was to be holy
as God is holy, then any deceit on her part would
tell other nations that her covenant Lord was
also deceitful instead of always trustworthy and
true. As Numbers 23:19 says, "God is not a man,
that he should lie; neither the son of man, that
he should repent: hath he said, and shall he not
do it? or hath he spoken, and shall he not make
it good?" When we examine the vertical element
of the ninth commandment, we see why Israel
needed to be a people committed to the truth.

The Connection to Christ and the Church

When we look into the Law we see not only the
attributes and righteousness of God the Father
but also the perfect righteousness and obedience
of Jesus Christ. If we divorce any commandment
from Christ, we will quickly find ourselves in
ethical quicksand. I think this is especially true of
the ninth commandment. Rather than beginning
with the Hebrew midwives who lied to Pharaoh

(Ex. 1:15–21) or with Rahab who lied to protect the Israelite spies (Josh. 2:4–6; Heb. 11:31) to determine whether it is ever permissible to lie, we should first look at the example of Christ. We know that Christ neither bore false witness nor lied but fulfilled every aspect of the Law. Christ was sinless; the Scriptures remind us that He was tempted in every way yet was without sin (Heb. 4:15). Christ's truthfulness is affirmed in several places in the New Testament.

For example, the apostle John says in Revelation that Christ is holy and true (Rev. 3:7) and is "the Amen, the faithful and true witness" (Rev. 3:14). Peter also affirms Christ's truthfulness in saying He "did no sin, neither was guile found in his mouth" (1 Pet. 2:22). The truthfulness of Christ is often contrasted with Satan, the father of lies. For example, Christ rebuked the Pharisees, saying, "Ye are of your father the devil, and the lusts of your father ye will do. He was a murderer from the beginning, and abode not in the truth, because there is no truth in him. When he speaketh a lie, he speaketh of his own: for he is a liar, and the father of it" (John 8:44). Jesus is the embodiment of the truth. He is trustworthy and never uttered a lie, whereas Satan does not possess truth and is the father of lies.

When we see that the Law finds its fulfillment in Jesus Christ and reflects the perfect righteousness of Christ, further implications of the Law become apparent. We have been redeemed from the dominion of sin and death and are daily being transformed into the image of Christ. We have been crucified and have left behind our old ways, including deceit. Paul explains this to the church at Ephesus:

> That ye put off concerning the former con-versation the old man, which is corrupt according to the deceitful lusts; and be re-newed in the spirit of your mind; and that ye put on the new man, which after God is created in righteousness and true holiness. Wherefore putting away lying, speak every man truth with his neighbour: for we are members one of another (Eph. 4:22–25).

When we are brought into the kingdom of Christ, we receive the Holy Spirit, whom Christ calls the Spirit of truth: "And I will pray the Father, and he shall give you another Comforter, that he may abide with you for ever; even the Spirit of truth; whom the world cannot receive, because it seeth him not, neither knoweth him: but ye know him; for he dwelleth with you, and shall be in you" (John 14:16–17). By contrast, the unbeliev-ing world embraces and lives in deceit. Paul says in the opening chapter of Romans that God gave up the wicked to the lusts of their hearts and to impurity because they exchanged the truth about God for a lie (Rom. 1:24–25). So, given that we are being remade and renewed into Christ's image, let us consider whether it is ever permissible to lie.

What theologians call *mendacium perniciosum*, or the malicious lie told out of evil motives, is clearly condemned in the Scriptures. We have also seen that Scripture speaks against *mendacium iocosum*, or a lie told for fun, saying one who tells it is like a madman who throws flaming arrows. What is not so clearly wrong is what theologians call the *mendacium officiosum*, or a lie of necessity, or an untruth that is told to protect others. Biblical examples of such deceit are the Hebrew midwives in Egypt (Ex. 1:15–22) and Rahab's protection of the Hebrew spies (Josh. 2:1–6). In more recent times people have asked: if we lived in Holland when the Nazis occupied it, would it have been sinful to lie to hide Jews?

In the case of the Hebrew midwives and Rahab, we must realize that we are looking at fallible, sinful people who, with good intentions and a desire to please God, nonetheless, gave an imperfect expression of faith. I believe Scripture commends the Hebrew midwives and Rahab for their faith but not the way in which their faith was manifest. So the author of Hebrews writes: "By faith the harlot Rahab perished not with them that believed not, when she had received the spies with peace" (Heb. 11:31). Note that the author does not commend Rahab for her lie but for her friendly welcome of the Israelite spies. Additionally, when we consider whether it was right to hide Jews from the Nazis, we should read Corrie Ten Boom's book *The Hiding Place* before answering this question. Corrie Ten Boom tells about how her sister, Nollie, told the truth to the Germans when questioned about hiding Jews. Nollie admitted they were hiding Jews, so the Jews were captured and taken to a theater to await transport to the concentration camps. Within hours of their capture, however, the Dutch resistance broke into the theater and freed the prisoners.[1]

In such cases we must ask ourselves whether we are trusting our own ability, and lying to protect ourselves and others, or whether we are seeking shelter in the providential hand and care of God. I believe that the lie of necessity carries with it the presupposition that God always wants us to remain safe. Though this is a perfectly understandable response, it is unbiblical. Human nature is prone to self-preservation. However, if we are to be conformed to the image of Christ, then suffering is not at odds with our calling. Nor should we as Christians lie to protect ourselves from suffering. Rather, we are called to suffer. That is what lies behind Peter's statement regarding Christ's truthfulness: "For even hereunto were ye called: because Christ also suffered for us, leaving us an example,

---

1. Corrie Ten Boom, *The Hidding Place* (Urichville: Barbour Publishing, 1961), 92–93, 111–12.

that ye should follow his steps: who did no sin, neither was guile found in his mouth: who, when he was reviled, reviled not again; when he suffered, he threatened not; but committed himself to him that judgeth righteously" (1 Pet. 2:21–23). So in cases where our lives are in danger, we should refuse to lie and remember that our calling is to speak the truth or remain silent as Christ did.

I suspect, however, that few of us will find ourselves in a life-or-death situation that presents us with the dilemma of whether we should lie to protect others or ourselves. What often happens is that the lie of necessity, which is rare and usually arises only in cases of life and death, is wrongly applied to other areas of life. Consider this example: A wife asks her husband, "Does this dress make me look fat?" The husband's mind races and he thinks, "I do not want her to be angry with me, nor do I want to deal with such an uncomfortable question, so I will lie." In such cases, we revert to our old nature, rather than speaking the truth according to the image of Christ. We are conformed to the patterns of this world rather than transformed by the renewing of our minds (Rom. 12:1–2).

In such circumstances, conditioned by the Spirit's gifts of patience, love, and gentleness, should we not tell the truth? Might the husband respond to his wife's question by saying, "Dear, that dress does not flatter you"? This imaginary scenario may seem trite and inconsequential. However, the more we become accustomed to lying in small things, the more we will default to deceit in the large things. What might begin as, "We're late because we had car trouble" to hide an argument between a husband and wife, might easily become, "I have to work late" to hide adultery. In every situation in life, we must strive to tell the truth in word or deed. Unfortunately, many Christians rarely tell a lie with their mouths but do so every day with their lives. On Sunday they profess to be Christians but throughout the workweek their conduct is no different from that of unbelievers. They may never utter a lie with their mouths but they lie with their lives.

Conclusion

When looking at the ninth commandment, we must realize its intense demand for truth in every situation in life. We may then mourn over our deceitfulness while fleeing to Christ, the one in whose mouth no deceit was found, the one who fulfilled every aspect of the Law and who bore its curse on our behalf. In light of our union with Christ, let us put away all deceit, for it has no part in our lives now that we are in Him and are being renewed in His image every day. Instead of looking at well-intentioned but fallible expressions of faith to determine whether we may lie, let us look to Jesus Christ and by the power of the Spirit strive to reflect His perfect righteousness and love.

STUDY QUESTIONS

1. Is the scope of the ninth commandment restricted merely to the courtroom setting?

2. Why is it important to look first to Christ rather than to Rahab or the Egyptian mid-wives to determine whether it is permissible to lie in order to preserve life?

3. What is a malicious lie (*mendacium perniciosum*)?

4. What is a lie told for fun (*mendacium iocosum*)?

5. What is a lie of necessity (*mendacium officiosum*)?

6. Who is the father of lies?

The Tenth Commandment

We see the actions of the people around us but seldom do we definitively know the motives behind them. We can only judge external appearances and at best make educated guesses about what lies beneath. The same cannot be said of God. God knows the heart of man. We cannot flee from His presence, whether in the heights or depths, or in life or death. God knows. The tenth commandment reminds us that God knows the motives of our actions; He knows whether we secretly covet the possessions of others even if we veil those covetous thoughts from others. The vertical element of this commandment, then, is clearly evident, but hopefully by keeping its historical, covenantal, and redemptive contexts in mind, our gaze will move from the Law to Christ and then to the way in which the Spirit applies this commandment to our lives.

In Its Original Setting

The tenth commandment says, "Thou shalt not covet thy neighbour's house, thou shalt not covet thy neighbour's wife, nor his manservant, nor his maidservant, nor his ox, nor his ass, nor any thing that is thy neighbour's" (Ex. 20:17). This commandment is somewhat unique in comparison to other laws governing the conduct of the Israelites. At least on the surface, commandments five through nine appear to deal with external conduct, whereas this commandment deals with motives of the heart. Yet that is only on the surface, because commandments five through nine, of course, also deal with motives of the heart. Let us see how this commandment affects the other nine.

When we read that the Israelites were forbidden to covet, we should understand that the term coveting means, "to desire or lust." In other words, coveting is not simply wanting something, but sinfully wanting something that we do not possess. The commandment then offers examples of what should not be coveted. A man should not lust after his neighbor's house, wife, servants, animals, or any of his possessions. In lusting after these things, desire can lead to the violation of other commandments. For example, in coveting the spouse of a neighbor, we not only violate the seventh commandment in thought but are tempted to violate it in action. When King David coveted Bathsheba, he went on to violate the seventh commandment by committing adultery with her, the eighth commandment by taking the wife of another man, and the sixth commandment by having Bathsheba's husband, Uriah the Hittite, killed.

Likewise, when King Ahab coveted Naboth's vineyard (1 Kings 21), he soon became guilty of violating other commandments. The king approved his wife Jezebel's plan to bear false witness against Naboth, saying that he had cursed the king (1 Kings 21:10). That was a violation of the ninth commandment. Ahab then had Naboth executed for his supposed curse, which was a violation of the sixth commandment (1 Kings 21:13). In the days of the prophet Amos, the merchants coveted wealth, which led them to violate the fourth, eighth, and ninth commandments (Amos 8:4–6). The tenth commandment has much to say about motives. In this regard, it is a unique commandment, for few cultures have laws that govern motives. Recognizing that the tenth commandment targets heart motives helps us to see that Christ was not raising the demands of the law in His Sermon on the Mount. Rather, by connecting the demands of the tenth commandment to the rest of the Law, Christ revealed that merely dealing with external behavior was not enough; the Law also dealt with motives of the heart. That is because violating the tenth commandment is often the gateway to violating the rest of the Law.

Let us probe deeper into this commandment

and explore how it relates to God. When we consider this vertical element, we must remember the covenantal context of this commandment, which is that God had promised to provide for all of Israel's needs. Specifically, God had promised to give Israel the Promised Land, with each Israelite household receiving a portion of the land. The inheritance of land is what kept Naboth from selling his property to King Ahab, for it had belonged to his fathers (1 Kings 21:4). If the Israelites recognized that everything they possessed was the result of God's kindness to them, they would be less inclined to covet what was not theirs. When the Israelites looked at the possessions of another and saw it as the blessing of God, they could not question the will or benevolence of God towards their neighbor. Moreover, the Israelites would realize that God had blessed them as well and they should be content with God's providence.

Notice that the commandment prohibits the coveting of earthly possessions. This should also clue us in to the vertical element of the commandment. The Israelites were commanded not to lust after earthly things but to recognize their transient nature. I think this heaven-ward focus is clearly evident in Abraham. By faith he left his home and traveled a great distance to live in the Promised Land. He lived in tents, not looking to his earthly possessions for comfort but ultimately to a city whose designer and builder was God

(Heb. 11:9–10). Abraham was looking for something far greater than the possessions and wealth of this world; he was looking for heaven itself. I think that setting our sights on something greater than our earthly possessions is the heart of the tenth commandment. Keeping this in mind, let us explore the connections between Christ and the church to the tenth commandment.

In the Light of Christ

When we look into the Law, we not only see the righteousness of God but also the perfect righteousness and love of Jesus Christ. In a familiar passage of Scripture, we see how Christ was content with His Father's will and set His sights beyond earthly possessions. Paul says Christ did not count equality with God a thing to be grasped but made Himself nothing. He took the form of a servant and humbled Himself by becoming obedient to the point of death, even death on a cross (Phil. 2:5–8). We have already looked at this passage of Scripture in considering the prohibition against stealing in the eighth commandment. Christ did not take or steal equality with God, as Adam attempted to do. I believe this reveals how the tenth commandment is connected to the other nine.

Christ's contentment with the will of His heavenly Father, which reflects His obedience to the tenth commandment, fueled His fulfillment of the eighth. Jesus did not covet what His heavenly

Father had not given Him. In the wilderness, Christ did not covet the food that Satan tempted Him to make, nor did He covet the glory that He might have received had He bowed the knee to Satan. Instead, He found contentment in the will of His Father (Matt. 4:4–10); He loved His Father more than food or power. At the same time, throughout His life Christ set His sights, not on earthly things, but upon heavenly things. When the time came for His crucifixion, resurrection, and ascension, Christ, "steadfastly set his face to go to Jerusalem" (Luke 9:51). Even in the depths of His anguish in the garden of Gethsemane, Christ set His heart to find contentment in the will of His Father, "Not as I will, but as thou wilt" (Matt. 26:39). Notice how Christ's contentment was manifest before Pilate. Jesus told Pilate, "My kingdom is not of this world: if my kingdom were of this world, then would my servants fight, that I should not be delivered to the Jews: but now is my kingdom not from hence" (John 18:36). Christ had His sight firmly fixed upon heavenly things, not upon earthly possessions, wealth, and transient glory. Because this was Christ's mindset, He obtained the name that is above every name (Phil 2:9–11).

Christ did not pursue the shortcut that Satan offered, to rule over all the nations, but instead was content to follow the will of His heavenly Father. He had His sight set on waiting for His Father to give Him rule over the nations. When we read the tenth commandment, then, we should not simply see a prohibition against coveting the possessions of others but instead see Christ's contentment in the will of His heavenly Father and His pursuit of heavenly things. This pattern must mark us as those who are being remade in the image of Christ and in whom the Spirit applies the rule of love.

The Connection to the Church

So often we find ourselves coveting the possessions of others. What lies at the root of our sin is a lack of contentment with God's will. We lust after what God has not given us, essentially slapping God across the face and crying out like a child, "More! I want more!" In the words of Paul, we are conformed to the patterns of this world (Rom. 12:1–2). Rather than feeding upon the manna from heaven, we feed upon commercials and advertisements of the world's table of possessions. While we cannot turn stones into bread, we can easily obtain many of the possessions we lust after by using a credit card.

What we do not realize is that we will never find satisfaction in things of this world. We will always look to the horizon, thinking that the object of our desire will deliver us from the lust for more. But our hearts can never be satisfied with things but can only be filled with God Himself. Augustine once wrote, "To praise you is the desire of man, a little piece of your creation. You stir man to take pleasure in praising you, because you have made us for yourself, and our heart is restless until it rests in you" (*Confessions*, 1.1). We will only find contentment and satisfaction in God and in His will.

Contentment in the will of our heavenly Father was the mindset of Christ as well as Paul, who wrote: "Not that I speak in respect of want: for I have learned, in whatsoever state I am, therewith to be content. I know both how to be abased, and I know how to abound: every where and in all things I am instructed both to be full and to be hungry, both to abound and to suffer need. I can do all things through Christ which strengtheneth me" (Phil. 4:11–13). Finding contentment in possessions is always fleeting because, as Augustine wrote, we were designed to find our contentment in Christ. Moreover, finding contentment in possessions or things is fleeting because things are of this world, not of the world to come.

For these reasons Christ instructs the church, "Lay not up for yourselves treasures upon earth, where moth and rust doth corrupt, and where thieves break through and steal: but lay up for yourselves treasures in heaven, where neither moth nor rust doth corrupt, and where thieves do not break through nor steal: for where your treasure is, there will your heart be also" (Matt. 6:19–21). If we truly hunger and thirst for the things of heaven, we will be like Abraham who looked to the heavenly city, and like Christ who looked to fulfill His Father's will and the praise of His Father for His obedience.

If we hunger and thirst for possessions, we will always be left wanting, whereas if we hunger and thirst for the things of heaven, we will be filled. Christ tells us that He is the bread of life and whoever comes to Him will not hunger, and whoever believes in Him will never thirst (John 6:35). In the Sermon on the Mount, Christ reminds us, "Blessed are they which do hunger and thirst after righteousness: for they shall be filled" (Matt. 5:6). If we seek satisfaction in Christ and His will, then no matter what the situation, our food will be to do the will of our heavenly Father, and His manna will satisfy us—we will covet no more (John 4:31–34).

Conclusion

When we hear the loud thunder of the Law, we should, like the Israelites, fear the Lord (Ex. 20:18–21). Moreover, we should realize the demands the tenth commandment levels against our covetous hearts. The tenth commandment clarifies that the Law was not merely legislation against external behavior as the Pharisees thought. Rather, the tenth commandment shows us that sin reflects motives such as a lack of contentment and seeking earthly rather than heavenly things. When we read the tenth commandment, we must listen intently to its accusation against our covetous desires, whatever they may be. Then we must behold Christ's contentment in His Father's will and His desire to set His sight upon heavenly things. When we consider the tenth commandment, then, we not only hear the prohibition against coveting but also the call for us to find contentment in Christ and to set our sights on the things of heaven. For only in Christ will we be satisfied and find fulfillment, rest, and peace. Therefore, by the power of the Spirit and our union with Christ we must seek first the kingdom of God and His righteousness, and all of our needs will be provided (Matt. 6:33–34).

STUDY QUESTIONS

1. In what way is the tenth commandment unique?

2. How is the tenth commandment related to the other nine?

3. How did Christ fulfill the tenth commandment?

4. Where do we find true contentment?

Conclusion

Having concluded our study of the Ten Commandments, I hope it is now evident how important it is to take into account the historical, covenantal, and redemptive contexts of the Law. The three most crucial rules of proper Bible interpretation are context, context, context! We must not forget that God revealed the Law to Israel in the historical context of the exodus from Egypt. Second, this redemption of Israel was a part of God's covenantal dealings with His people, which were made clear in His covenantal promises to Abraham, Isaac, and Jacob. Third, we take a step back from the immediate historical context of the Law to see the grand panorama of redemptive history and how all of the covenants find fulfillment in Christ. To approach the Law apart from Christ brings only death and condemnation.

Too many people look at the Law as only a list of things that they can do. They either look

at the Law as their means of salvation or as the
power behind their sanctification. If we recognize
the three important contexts of the Law, we will
see that the perfect obedience and righteousness of
Christ even unto death is what frees us from the
curse of the Law. We will also see that the Law
reflects God's holy attributes and character as well
as the perfect righteousness of Christ. Because we
are in union with Christ, we too are called upon
to reflect His holiness, righteousness, and love.

If we recognize that we must first look to Christ
when we hear the Law's condemnation of our sin,
we will receive the greatest hope and assurance
knowing that our standing before God is secure.
As Paul says, "But that no man is justified by
the law in the sight of God, it is evident: for the
just shall live by faith" (Gal. 3:11). That is we are
declared righteous in God's sight by faith alone in
Christ alone by God's grace alone. Through Christ
and the Spirit, however, we are enabled to fulfill
the Law: "For what the law could not do, in that
it was weak through the flesh, God sending his
own Son in the likeness of sinful flesh, and for sin,
condemned sin in the flesh: that the righteousness
of the law might be fulfilled in us, who walk not
after the flesh, but after the Spirit" (Rom. 8:3–4).
Because of who we are in Christ, we can manifest
the righteousness of the Law. As Paul says, "Owe
no man any thing, but to love one another: for
he that loveth another hath fulfilled the law. For

this, Thou shalt not commit adultery, Thou shalt not kill, Thou shalt not steal, Thou shalt not bear false witness, Thou shalt not covet; and if there be any other commandment, it is briefly comprehended in this saying, namely, Thou shalt love thy neighbour as thyself. Love worketh no ill to his neighbour: therefore love is the fulfilling of the law" (Rom. 13:8–10).

We now see the Christ-centered nature of the Law. If more Christians understood these truths, might more believers become more intimate in their knowledge of it? Might more Christians march in protest against the absence of the law, not in the courthouse, but in the church in public worship? Might parents be more concerned about whether their children are in union with Christ and have the Law written upon their hearts by the all-powerful work of the Holy Spirit than with debates about posting the Ten Commandments in public schools? Who needs the Ten Commandments in schools when covenant youth bear witness through their words and deeds not only of the Law of God but of the gospel of Christ and how He has fulfilled the Law? Might more Christians grow in their sanctification if they understood that the Law is powerless to save and sanctify, that it only condemns and shows us our need for Christ, and that it is Christ through the Spirit who saves and sanctifies?

Let us meditate upon the Law, teach it to our covenant children, talk of it when we are in our homes and when we walk by the way, think upon it when we lie down and when we rise from our slumber. As we do, may we see our sinfulness as the rule of love broken. May we recognize the glorious work of Christ our Savior as the rule of love fulfilled. May we experience the sanctifying power of the Spirit and show forth His holiness and righteousness, having the rule of love applied. Pray that, through Christ's application of the Law by the Holy Spirit, we would love the Lord our God with all our hearts, souls, and strength, and our neighbor as ourselves. *Soli Deo Gloria*!

STUDY QUESTIONS

1. What are the Ten Commandments? Can you list them from memory in order, including the prologue?

2. Why is faith in Christ vital to a proper use of the Law in the Christian life?

3. What is the role of the Law in our justification?

4. Our holiness comes from the Law, true or false?

5. Who writes the Law upon our hearts?

Scripture Index

Joel
2:32 24, 48

Amos
8:4–6 125

Habakkuk
1:11 26

Zechariah
5:4 47

Malachi
1:6 72

NEW TESTAMENT

Matthew
4:1–11 107
4:4–10 128
4:9–10 27
5:6 131
5:17 85, 107
5:22 84
5:27–28 92
5:31–32 93
5:43–48 87
6:19–21 130
6:24 26
6:33–34 132
10:37–38 26
11:28 64
22:37 29
22:37–39 70, 71
22:39 70, 112
26:39 74, 128
26:42 28

Luke
4:18–21 63
4:26 77
9:51 128
23:34 86

John
1:45 8
4:24 34
4:31–34 131
6:35 131
8:44 86, 115
8:48–49 74
14:6 23
14:8–9b 38
14:15 5
14:16–17 116
17:4 5, 62
18:36 128
19:30 62

Acts
2:21 24
2:23 85
4:11–12 24

Romans
1:22–23 25, 37
1:24–25 116
1:26–27 37
5:1–8 85
5:6–8 87
5:14 37
6:23 60
7:1–4 96
7:12 16
8:1–4 4
8:3–4 134

8:29 75
9:5 24
10:4 3
10:13–17 49
12:1–2 119, 129
13:8–10 135
16:25–26a 96

1 Corinthians
5:7 12
15:56 3

2 Corinthians
3:18 40
4:4 38

Galatians
3:11 134
3:12–14 14
3:13 86
3:16 11, 20, 31
3:18–19b 14
3:18–26 16
3:23–24 14

Ephesians
4:22–25 116
4:26 85
5:18 76
5:21 76
5:22 75
5:25–27 95
5:25–30 24
5:28–32 95
6:1–3 75
6:5 75

Philippians
2:5 108
2:5–8 74, 127
2:5–11 27, 38, 107
2:6 107
2:8 74, 107
2:9–11 48, 128
3:19 26
4:11–13 130

Colossians
1:13–14 12, 20, 31
2:16–17 61
3:9–10 86

1 Timothy
1:8–10 102

Titus
2:2–5 51
2:9–10 109

Hebrews
1:1–2a 23
1:3 38
4:15 85, 115
8:6–7 11
10:12–13 62
11:9–10 127
11:31 115, 117
12:24 12

James
2:8 16
2:10 85
3:9 84